Mich Turner's
Cake School

Mich Turner's Cake School

Expert Tuition from the Master Cake Maker

MICH TURNER MBE

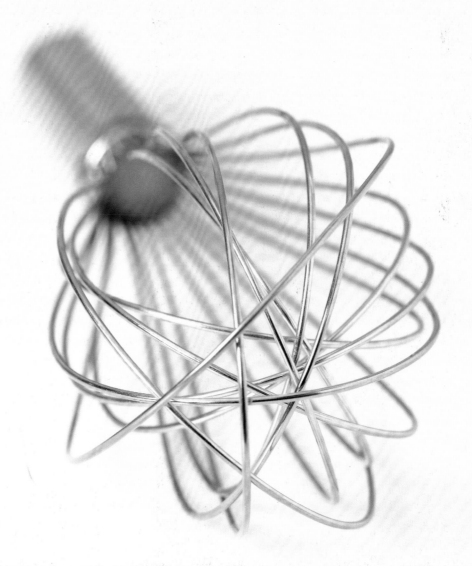

jacqui
small

For my boys Phil, Marlow and George

First published in 2014 by
Jacqui Small LLP
An imprint of Aurum Press
74–77 White Lion Street
London N1 9PF

Publisher: Jacqui Small
Managing Editor: Lydia Halliday
Art Director: Ashley Western
Photographer: Amanda Heywood
Project Editor: Abi Waters
Production: Maeve Healey

ISBN: 978 1 909342 22 4

A catalogue record for this book is available from the British Library.

2016 2015 2014
10 9 8 7 6 5 4 3 2 1

Printed in China

Contents

Introduction

I have made cakes all my life and have discovered there are those who can bake and those who think they can't. I take this as a challenge – as it is only when I drill down into their methodology that the root of their failings becomes apparent and I can offer practical advice and a solution to set them off on the road to success.

In *Cake School*, I call upon my 25 years of experience in the industry and my knowledge as a qualified food scientist to provide the tools, tutorials and tuition to inspire your creativity and ensure guaranteed success every time you make and bake a cake.

This book is intended to do more than just provide recipes. It is about helping you to understand what is happening at each stage of cake making and why these steps are important; learning these fundamentals will ensure many years of successful cake making. Whether you are a complete novice or an experienced professional baker, I have discovered there is always more to learn.

Throughout my book I offer tips, hints, practical advice, what to do, what not to do and highlight the key stages and critical points. I break each stage down into manageable tasks. It is essential to take time when making cakes, using the best quality fresh ingredients – I can often be heard chanting 'You can't make a silk purse from a sow's ear!'

There is a real art and science to making cakes and with the knowledge I am sharing with you in this book, I hope you too will be inspired to make, bake, fill, frost, ice and decorate. Enjoy your time at Cake School.

Mich Turner MBE

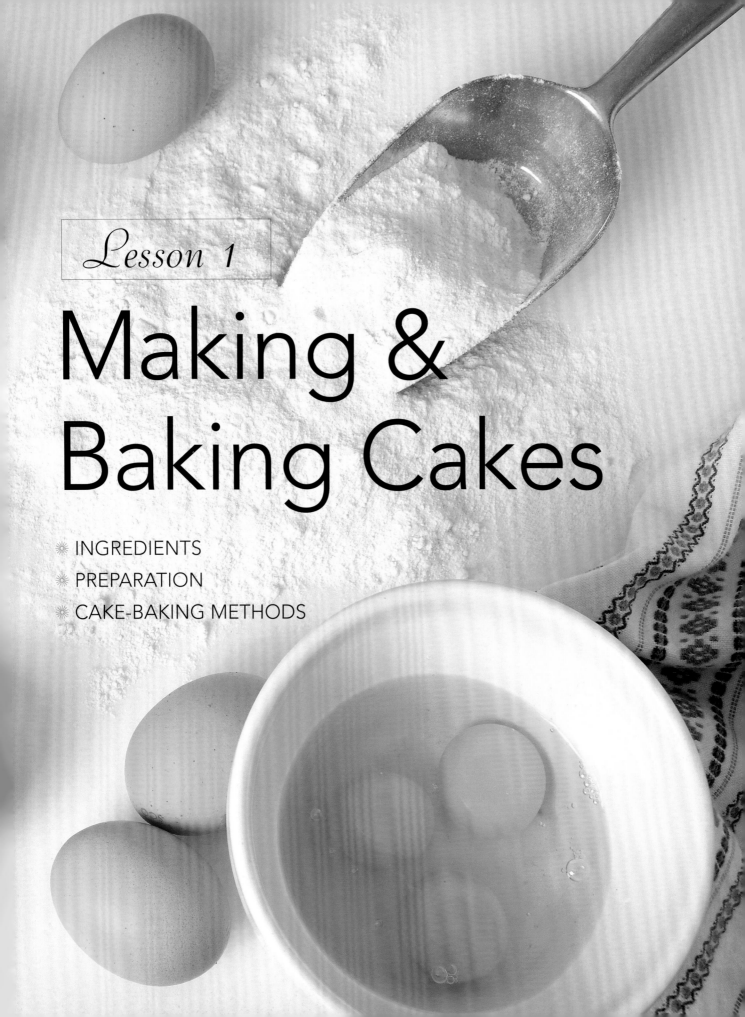

Making & Baking Cakes

* INGREDIENTS
* PREPARATION
* CAKE-BAKING METHODS

Ingredients

A great cake is made using the **finest quality**, freshest ingredients. I am a firm believer in over-emphasizing **flavours** so they really **pack a punch** and satisfy the palate without having to have an enormous slice. Use **local** and **seasonal** ingredients to transform cakes into something **truly special** and experiment with one ingredient to make it a 'hero' of your chosen cake. Once you have mastered the **fundamentals** of cake making, substituting different ingredients and sugars can subtly **transform** and **personalize** your cakes.

Sugars

Sugar is the backbone of every cake – but the many different types available can encourage subtle differences to your baked cakes. Sugar is obtained either from the sugar cane or sugar beet. There is no difference between the two. Experiment to see which type of sugar you prefer.

White or Refined Sugars

Refined sugars are pure, white and are valued for their quick-dissolving properties. Refined sugars have been treated to remove the molasses. The white, refined sugars will add pure sweetness, a more crispy texture and a paler colour to the end result.

White icing sugar I use this for making pure white buttercream. The neutral base colour is ideal when adding additional fruit purées or colours to achieve controlled shades. This sugar is also the base for royal icing, glacé icing and fondant as it achieves the perfect blank canvas for all additional decoration.

✔ IDEAL FOR royal icing and white buttercream.

Unrefined icing sugar This icing sugar makes the best buttercream – it has a more caramelized flavour rather than just being sweet, and a golden caramel colour. Use this sugar to add a wonderful flavour to meringue. This icing sugar can be used in royal icing, glacé icing and fondant to create a frosting that will have a wonderful natural caramel colour and flavour.

✔ IDEAL FOR buttercream and naturally coloured royal icing.

Caster sugar (castor sugar / superfine sugar) White caster sugar is used for making a pure white Italian meringue and is used in cakes to give a crispy texture and sweet flavour.

✔ IDEAL FOR Italian meringue.

Golden caster sugar I tend to use this sugar in all my softer, white cakes such as the vanilla (see pages 44–45), lemon (see page 91) and chiffon (see page 62). It creams beautifully with butter and has the benefit of being light with an element of chewy caramel, which adds moistness and flavour to the baked cakes.

✔ IDEAL FOR cake making and Swiss meringue buttercream.

> White sugars will add a crunchy short bite, while the brown sugars will add a depth of flavour and a chewy texture.

Glucose Syrup

Molasses or Black Treacle

Golden Caster Sugar

Unrefined Icing Sugar

White Icing Sugar

MICH'S TIP

Be careful to avoid product simply labelled 'brown sugar,' which is a flavoured, coloured refined white sugar with none of the nutritional benefits of the unrefined. The unrefined sugars will always state the country of origin on the packet and offer a more caramelized, rounded flavour, chewy texture and a darker bake. Experiment with blending different sugars when you make and bake cakes to find your personal favourite combinations.

Brown or Unrefined Sugars

These sugars include demerara, light brown and muscovado. They have different uses in cake making but are all unrefined, retaining essential nutritional value with differing amounts of molasses. They can be made from sugar cane or sugar beet.

Light soft brown sugar I use this in all my chocolate base cakes – being naturally darker the colour does not affect the overall baked cake. The sugar adds a wonderful caramel flavour with an intense chewy texture, which works beautifully in a chocolate cake.
✔ IDEAL FOR melted method cakes and chocolate based cakes.

Dark soft brown sugar / muscovado sugar This sugar contains a high percentage of molasses, which will ensure the cakes are rich, dark, intensely flavoured and moist. The sugar tends to be used in spiced cakes to balance the flavours – such as sticky gingerbread (see page 73) and indulgent rich fruit cake (see page 74).
✔ IDEAL FOR rich fruit and spiced cakes.

Liquid Sugars

Honey I find it best to use honey for additional flavour rather than as a sweetener per se. Added to crumble toppings or fillings it can add depth, but is not generally used as the base for cake making.
✔ IDEAL FOR adding flavour to buttercreams and cakes.

Maple syrup Be sure to use the real maple syrup, which is quite thin and runny and is formed from the sap of maple trees and not maple-flavoured syrup, which tends to be much sweeter and more viscous. It adds a subtle flavour to baked cakes, but comes into its own when used as a flavour in fillings and frostings.
✔ IDEAL FOR fillings and frostings.

Glucose syrup This invert sugar is a clear sugar that is liquid at room temperature. Readily available, it adds lubrication to fillings and frostings such as ganache, meringue and honeycomb.
✔ IDEAL FOR chocolate ganache and royal icing.

Golden syrup or pale treacle This golden pale viscous syrup is made from the syrup that remains after sugar is refined. It can be used for making frostings, glazes, honeycomb and chocolate biscuit cake as well as many puddings.
✔ IDEAL FOR frostings, glazes and honeycomb.

Black treacle or molasses This uncrystallized dark syrup is the almost-black residue gathered from the latter stages of sugar refining once sugar has been removed, and is less sweet than other treacles. It has a thick, viscous consistency, and is rich in B vitamins and minerals, especially iron. It gives an intense dark colour, burnt caramel flavour and moisture to baked cakes.
✔ IDEAL FOR spiced cakes.

Honey

Light Brown Sugar

Dark Brown/Muscovado Sugar

Flours

Most cakes are made with wheat flour which provides starch and protein (gluten) to support the structure of the cake. As the cake bakes the starch granules swell, burst and absorb the moisture in the cake batter. The protein (gluten) stretches around the air pockets and denatures at high temperature, supporting the honeycomb structure of the baked cake.

Types of Flour

White wheat flour will provide the best result for cakes – light, aerated with sufficient starch and protein to support the cake and absorb the moisture during baking.

✔ IDEAL FOR all types of cakes and biscuits.

Wholemeal flour will contain all of the wheat grain and offers additional nutrition. This flour works well in melted method cakes, where there is a lot of moisture and strong flavours from spices and sugars. Cakes made with wholemeal flour tend to be more dense, with less aeration, and require more moisture before baking; but can offer a greater depth of flavour and texture.

✔ IDEAL FOR root vegetable cakes.

Plain flour will be pure wheat flour with no raising agents added.

✔ IDEAL FOR whisked and chocolate cakes.

Self-raising flour has baking powder already included in with the flour. Barley and spelt (an ancient variety of wheat) flours can be substituted in part for wheat flour to add texture and flavour, but are less readily available, and will give different results as they are lower in gluten.

✔ IDEAL FOR all-in-one method and creamed cakes.

Polenta milled from maize / corn is gluten free and can be used in cakes either combined with almonds for a totally gluten-free cake, or with wheat flour to provide interesting texture, colour and added nutrition.

✔ IDEAL FOR gluten-free cakes or to add colour and texture.

Gluten-free flour can be milled from rice, corn, tapioca, buckwheat or potato and can be substituted successfully in cake baking where the recipe requires a lower percentage of flour, and has other strong flavours included – such as chocolate, spices and treacle. The effect of using gluten-free flour tends to be more crumbly with a gritty texture and stronger aftertaste. Xanthan gum can be added to cakes made with gluten-free flour to improve the crumb structure and reduce crumbling.

✔ IDEAL FOR gluten-free cakes.

"My golden rule is that cakes should always be made with an all-purpose wheat flour that is lower in gluten and never with strong bread flour as it will result in tough, chewy, dense cakes."

Flour should be stored in an airtight container away from moisture and humidity to prevent it clumping. Use self-raising flour within its use-by date as the potency of the raising agent will diminish over time.

Fats

Fats add flavour and mouthfeel to cakes and bakes, and will improve the keeping qualities of the cake. They can be added in solid (butter, lard, margarine) or liquid form (oils). Make sure all fats and oils are at room temperature to maximize creaming.

Butter – the most common fat used in cake making, made up of minimum 80% fat. Butter can be unsalted or salted and while either will give the same physical results the flavour will be different. I prefer to use unsalted butter in all my baking, adding a dash of salt to specific recipes if I think they benefit. Unsalted butter has a wonderfully clean, lactic taste and this blends beautifully in cakes and bakes. Always ensure the butter is fresh and allowed to come up to room temperature naturally.

✔ IDEAL FOR creaming cakes and buttercream.

Margarine – these are also minimum 80% fat and manufactured from vegetable-based oils that have been hydrogenated to turn them from a liquid to a solid at room temperature and are therefore high in trans fats. Nutritionally, they offer no benefit over butter. They are softer at room temperature and can therefore cream well. They have less flavour than butter and although can also be less expensive they cannot be as readily digested in the body.

✔ IDEAL FOR all-in-one method cakes.

Oils – these are 100% fat and are liquid at room temperature. These oils are great for melted method cakes and batter and foam cakes. They will help to keep the baked cake moist, which can be refrigerated successfully as the oils will still remain soft. Canola, sunflower and rapeseed are all successful for baking as individuals oils; or use vegetable oil which is a blend. Groundnut has little if any flavour or taste and is good for lining tins.

✔ IDEAL FOR chiffon and root vegetable cakes.

Lard – this is a solid fat that is 100% pig fat. It is great as a shortening for pastry and can be used for steamed puddings but I would not recommend it for making cakes – it does not cream well. It is worth noting that despite its reputation, lard has less saturated fat, more unsaturated fat and less cholesterol than butter by weight.

✔ IDEAL FOR pastry.

> *" I prefer to use unsalted butter in all my baking, adding a dash of salt to specific recipes if I think they benefit. "*

Cakes made with butter or margarine will become firmer and taste drier if stored and eaten directly from the refrigerator, as the fat inside will be solid when chilled. Leave to come up to room temperature.

Eggs

Eggs are used extensively in making cakes as they have a compound effect on the baked structure of the cake. Egg yolk contains a moisturizing fat and lecithin – an effective emulsifying agent. This emulsifier will help to keep the cake batter stable to create a cake with an even texture.

Egg white is an elasticated protein. It has the ability to aerate and trap a large volume of tiny air bubbles which can then be incorporated into the cake. As the cake bakes, the egg white protein will set firm, trapping these air bubbles resulting in a light-as-air cake. This is why it is essential to use fresh eggs at room temperature. They will have better elasticity for maximum aeration.

It is important to use fresh eggs well within their sell-by date. Their structure, composition and ability to function reduces over their life. Over time the air sac inside the egg will increase and the egg will be less dense and will float if placed in a bowl of cold water. Egg shells are porous and will pick up any strong flavours they are stored near to. Eggs should be kept inside the egg box, refrigerated, and then allowed to come up to room temperature overnight before using in cake making.

Hen eggs are the most readily available – my recipes have been developed using either medium or large. Medium eggs weigh between 53–63g (1¾–2¼oz) Large eggs weigh between 63–73g (2¼–2½ oz).

Duck eggs can be substituted in making the lighter vanilla cakes. They have a higher fat content so the cakes will be fluffy, moist and light.

Goose eggs can also be used in baking, offering a rich, creamy, light texture. As a rule of thumb substitute 1 goose egg for 3 hens' eggs.

It is now possible to obtain pasteurized egg white – available from the chilled section of supermarkets. The carton contains the equivalent of 15 egg whites which can be used safely in making meringue and royal icing.

✔ ALL EGGS ARE IDEAL FOR cake making.

MICH'S TIP

To check if an egg is fresh place it in a bowl of cold water. If the egg sinks it will be fresh and can be used. If an egg floats or the base of the egg gravitates towards the surface these should be discarded.

❝ *I always remove eggs from the fridge at least 6 hours (or ideally overnight) before baking to ensure they come up to room temperature.* ❞

Additional ingredients

In addition to the basic ingredients, cakes can be packed with a whole host of nutritious, exciting fruits, vegetables, nuts and spices. Try embellishing your favourite cakes to expand your repertoire.

Fruits

Fresh seasonal fruits are a wonderful addition to cake making. They can be baked into cakes adding colour, flavour and texture. Citrus zests and juices can be used to enhance flavours and create delicious, flavourful syrups and candied peel. Soft fruits and berries can be used to create wonderful compotes and purées or used for visual decoration.

Dried fruits can be used to enhance the intensity, flavour, moisture and nutritional content of cakes. Common vine fruits include currants, sultanas and raisins, but dried cherries, cranberries, dates, figs, prunes and apricots can make wonderful additions to cakes. Try experimenting to find your favourite combinations.

Vegetables

Carrot cake is now a regular feature in most coffee shops, cafés and bakeries but other vegetables can also be considered to create deliciously nutritious, wonderfully moist, less sweet cakes. Vegetables contain lots of essential minerals and vitamins, little or no fat and are lower in sugar. Courgettes, beetroot, sweet potato and parsnip can all be used to make fabulous cakes.

Nuts

Nuts are a rich source of protein and essential oils. They add great texture and flavour to cakes and can be used additionally in fillings and frostings and for decoration.

Chocolate

Unquestionably the most indulgent of all additional ingredients to be used in cake making. There are many chocolates available but the essential ones for cake making are plain and white.

Plain chocolate (70% cocoa solids) Labelling of chocolate as a percentage cocoa solids generally refers to the total combined amount of cocoa solids and cocoa butter. Additional ingredients will include sugar, milk, lecithin and vanilla. The higher the percentage of cocoa solids and the lower the sugar content will be an indication of the quality and intensity of the chocolate flavour. For all my cake making I use chocolate labelled 70% cocoa solids – less than this will deliver a lacklustre chocolate flavour; more than this will be too bitter.

White chocolate is technically not real chocolate as it doesn't contain any cocoa solids. It is a combination of cocoa butter, sugar and a minimum of 14% milk solids, with 3–5% milk fat. Vanilla is added for flavour. It doesn't have the strength of dark chocolate to be used in baking a cake, but can add a delectably light creaminess to buttercreams, ganaches and decorations.

"For all my cake making I use chocolate labelled 70% cocoa solids. Less than this will deliver a lacklustre chocolate flavour; more than this will be too bitter."

Making & Baking Cakes 19

Spices, flavours & alcohols

While a cake is made essentially from the core ingredients – flour, fat, sugar and egg – it is the additional flavourings, spices and embellishments that truly make the cake identifiable and memorable.

Flavourings

Vanilla is one of the most widely used flavours in cake making. It is available in a variety of formats, making it convenient for specific purposes. Vanilla pods contain the seeds from the air root of the vanilla orchid plant.

Vanilla pod – split and scrape a vanilla pod at the time you use it for an intense concentration of flavour. Place the discarded vanilla pod in a jar of caster sugar to make your own vanilla sugar for use in other bakes and for adding flavourful decoration.

Vanilla bean paste – a spoonable, viscous liquid containing the vanilla seeds. This paste is easy to measure and delivers an authentic black speckled hit of vanilla packed with flavour. I like to use this in buttercreams and vanilla cakes.

Vanilla extract – a brown liquid that will deliver flavour without any of the black speckled seeds. Good for darker coloured cakes where the seeds would not be seen – such as chocolate or fruit. This is less expensive than the vanilla pods or vanilla bean pastes.

Other flavours such as rose water, orange blossom water, orange oil, almond extract and peppermint oil are all available and can deliver a great intensity or delicate hint of flavour.

Spices

Many spices can be used in baking including cinnamon, nutmeg, cloves, ginger and cardamom. Ginger may be freshly grated, dried ground, stem or crystallized, delivering a wonderful distinctive potency.

MICH'S TIP

Buy your spices in small quantities and store in separate sealed bags; they lose their potency quickly once opened. Use a new bag every time you make the recipe to ensure the spices are fresh.

Bicarbonate of Soda   Vanilla Pods   Rose Water   Cinnamon Sticks

Crystallized Ginger   Ground Ginger   Cloves

> *"I am not a lover of overly alcoholic cakes but I do like to use alcohols to soak fruits prior to baking to add a wonderful depth."*

Alcohol

I am not a lover of overly alcoholic cakes but I do like to use alcohols to soak fruits prior to baking to add a wonderful depth of flavour and moistness to my cakes.

Brandy, rum and sherry can all be used to soak vine fruits. Kirsch has a wonderful affinity with cherries – whether they are fresh, dried or morello.

Champagne can be added to fresh berries for an indulgent summer fruit compote. Guinness or stout can be used in rich decadent cakes combined with chocolate or indulgent fruits.

Raising Agents & Chemical Salts

These are responsible for the organic chemistry that happens in cake making.

Baking powder – a raising agent containing bicarbonate of soda and tartaric acid, usually with an anti-caking starch to absorb moisture during storage and help keep the powder free-flowing. These chemicals produce carbon dioxide when they come into contact with moisture, which helps the cake to rise.

Bicarbonate of soda or sodium bicarbonate is a white crystalline solid ground to a fine powder. It has a slightly salty, alkaline taste, which when it comes into contact with an acid will react and produce carbon dioxide, which then works as a raising agent. Such acids will include lemon juice, vinegar, buttermilk and yoghurt.

Cream of tartar – potassium hydrogen tartrate is produced as a by-product of wine making. The fine crystals are derived from refined tartaric acid, which forms on the inside of wine barrels. It is added to sodium bicarbonate to form commercial baking powder. It can be used by itself for stabilizing egg whites, increasing their heat resistance and increasing their volume when making meringues or foams.

Kirsch

Stout

Rum

Brandy

Vanilla Bean Paste

Nutmeg

White Chocolate Chips

Dark Chocolate Chips

Stem Ginger

Cocoa Powder

Preparation

It is important to allocate sufficient time to **prepare** for making and baking cakes. All ingredients should be **fresh**, weighed accurately and left to come up to room **temperature** where recommended. All bowls and **equipment** should be **scrupulously clean** and the right tool selected for the task. Bowls should be large enough to accommodate the aeration during creaming and whisking. Tins should be **measured** accurately and lined **carefully** to ensure a **professionally** baked cake.

Lining baking tins

Lining tins can be a mundane, time-consuming job, but it is so important to line properly and accurately. This will ensure the cake bakes well with a clean, well formed shape that can then be easily removed from the tin. Always line the tins before you start making the cake to ensure it is ready as soon as the cake batter is.

LINING A ROUND, SQUARE OR SHAPED DEEP-SIDED TIN
(7.5cm/3 inch depth or greater)

Fold a sheet of non-stick baking parchment in half. Place the tin on top and draw around the outside of the tin using a pencil. Holding the folded sheet of baking parchment, carefully cut out 2 shapes just inside the pencil template. Fold another sheet of non-stick baking parchment in half lengthways and turn the folded edge up 2.5cm (1 inch) all the way along and press to form a crease.

MICH'S TIPS

1 The sheet of baking parchment should be just slightly longer than the circumference of the tin, and be 2.5cm (1 inch) above the height of the tin. Measure the circumference with a tape measure or length of string or ribbon. For larger tins you may well need to use more than one length of baking parchment to line the full way around the tin.

2 It can be helpful to brush a little sunflower oil over the base and sides of the tin before inserting the non-stick baking parchment to hold it in position.

3 Commercial Bake-O-Glide can be cut to fit and re-used if you bake a certain size of cake on a regular basis.

Use a sharp pair of scissors to cut diagonal slits along the folded edge up to the crease, at 2.5cm (1 inch) intervals. Place one base sheet in the base of the tin and insert the side liner(s) and press to fit. Place the other base sheet inside the tin. This will cover the diagonal cuts on the side liner, ensuring the cake batter does not bake into the pleats. The tin is now ready for use.

It is important for cake batter to be transferred into the tin and placed in a hot oven as soon as it is mixed to make the most of the active raising agent and aeration.

LINING A BAKING TRAY, SWISS ROLL TIN OR BROWNIE TRAY

Place the tin on a sheet of non-stick baking parchment allowing for a 5–7.5cm (2–3 inch) border around the edge – this border is for the depth of the sides of the tin. Draw around the base of the tin with a pencil. Cut the corners off the baking parchment, coming from each top and side edge of the baking parchment to reach the pencil line. The resulting paper should be rectangular with 4 square corners cut out. Fold along the pencil lines to form a sharp crease. Place the prepared liner inside the tin.

Even non-stick tins benefit from being lined to add protection to the gentle crumb structure of the cake as it is removed and handled.

LINING A BUNDT MOULD OR KUGELHOPF TIN

There are many aerosol sprays available that can deliver an even coat of grease. These are particularly useful for intricate formed tins and silicone moulds.

LINING A RING MOULD

Brush the inside of the tin with melted butter, making sure to cover all areas evenly. Sprinkle enough flour inside the tin to coat the base and sides. Gently tap and rotate the tin until the base and all internal sides are dusted. Turn the tin upside down and tap to remove any excess flour. The tin is now ready to use.

LINING A TIN FOR NON-BAKING

Some cakes are not baked, but are set in a fridge. These cakes are placed in tins lined with cling film. Brush the tin with sunflower or groundnut oil and press sheets of cling film into the tin until all sides and the base are covered. The tin is now ready to use.

Removing cakes from tins

Once a cake is baked it is essential to know how it should be cooled and when and how to safely remove it from the tin to protect the delicate crumb structure. This will help to prevent it from collapsing, drying out or becoming soggy and dense. It is always a good idea to use an oven cloth or mitts to safely handle hot cake tins as they are removed from the oven. Preparation is key – cakes will be removed easily from the tins if they have been properly lined before baking.

REMOVING FROM A TIN

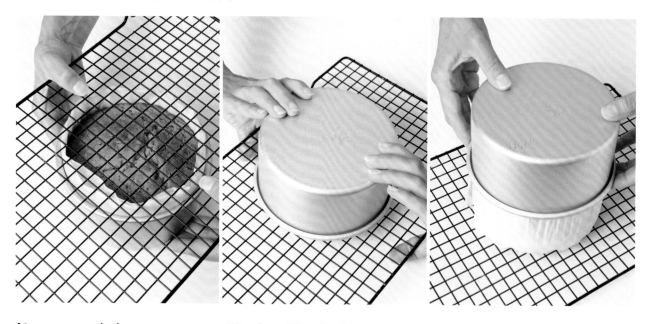

Use an oven cloth to remove the cake from the oven and place on a wire rack. Leave the cake to cool completely – this will depend on the size of the cake, but generally allow for 4 hours. Place a wire rack, upside down, on top of the tin.

Firmly holding both cake tin and rack, invert them together. Carefully lift the tin off the cake, keeping the sides straight as you go.

MICH'S TIP

Many cakes need to cool in the tin to firm up and retain moisture. Removing cakes too early allows the steam to rapidly escape resulting in a drier cake and runs the risk of the cake collapsing under its own weight. There are always exceptions and these are highlighted throughout the book.

Remove the baking parchment from the sides of the cake. Carefully peel back the non-stick parchment that is lining the base of the cake. Place a cake board on the visible surface (base) of the cake and, using the wire rack, turn the cake back over to the right way up. Remove the wire rack.

"*Invest in a cooling rack large enough to support your baked cakes. I usually turn super-sized cakes out onto cake boards.*"

REMOVING FROM A SPRINGFORM TIN

Run a sharp knife around the inside edge of the tin to loosen the cake. Release the spring clip on the outside of the tin.

Carefully lift the tin away from the cake. Slide the cake off the base of the tin. Turn the cake over (a small cake can be held in your hands, or use a cake board to assist and support if necessary) and peel back the non-stick lining.

REMOVING FROM A RING MOULD

Allow the cake to cool with the tin suspended over an upturned glass bowl. This allows the steam to escape without crushing the cake. Run a palette knife around the inside edge of the tin to loosen the cake. Firmly hold the cake tin and gently push the inner liner up and out to release the cake.

Depending on the cake you are making, some need to cool in the tin, while others should be removed immediately. Handling hot, heavy cakes can be difficult. Invest in a good pair of oven gloves and a selection of wire racks.

REMOVING A ROULADE FROM A TIN

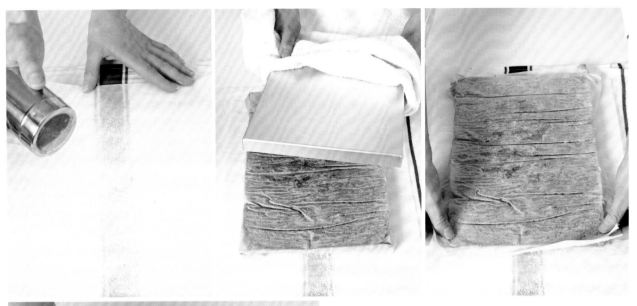

Place a sheet of non-stick baking parchment on a clean damp tea towel on a work surface. Sprinkle with golden caster sugar or icing sugar. As soon as the cake is baked remove from the oven and upturn it onto the non-stick baking parchment.

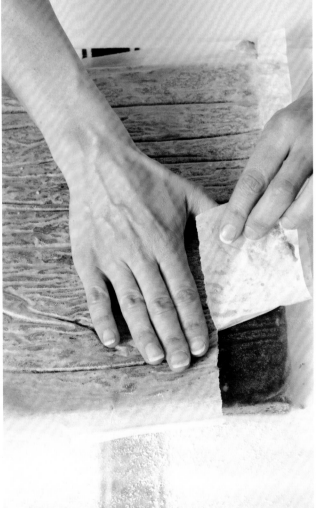

Make sure all the corners of the paper are untucked. Peel the paper away in strips being careful to protect the surface of the roulade.

"Handling hot, heavy cakes straight from the oven requires care and diligence."

Cake-baking Methods

There are many methods of cake making to master and the varying methods will result in cakes with different eating, handling and storage properties. In this cake-baking section I will show you the basic methods for creaming, whisking, melted and all-in-one methods, focussing on the key stages in each method. I will also highlight the pitfalls that are best avoided to ensure you achieve consistent and successful baking every time.

1   The Creamed Cake Method

2   The Whisked Cake Method

3   The Batter & Foam Method

4   The All-in-one Method

5   The Melted Method

1 The Creamed Cake Method

Creaming involves beating softened butter or margarine and sugar together with an electric whisk until the emulsion is light, aerated and voluminous. Eggs are added very slowly, beating well between each addition to create a stable emulsion (the lecithin in the egg yolk) with maximum aeration (the albumen – the elastic egg white protein). Flour is folded in with a light touch and a metal spoon or flat-blade spatula to avoid knocking out all the air.

INGREDIENTS

This sequence provides step-by-step instructions on the method of making a creamed cake. There is no standard recipe, but most will use softened unsalted butter, golden caster sugar, eggs, plain flour and can also have additional flavouring added in the form of vanilla bean paste, citrus zest or chocolate etc.

Please see specific recipes for measurements, oven temperatures and baking times.

All ingredients (with the exception of the milk) should be at room temperature.

Place the softened butter and sugar in the clean bowl of a kitchen mixer. Turn the mixer on slow speed at first to incorporate the butter and sugar together. Continue to cream on high speed for up to 10 minutes to achieve the perfect creamed cake.

✕ What not to do

Not creaming for long enough will prevent the batter from having sufficient air incorporated into the cake – this will result in the cake being dense, tough, with lower sides and a peak in the centre of the cake.

✗ What not to do

Adding the eggs too quickly will split the batter. This does not affect the flavour but the cake will be less aerated and stabilized resulting in a more dense cake. If the creaming and egg stages have been hurried, the batter will be runny and curdled. Overcome this by adding 1 tablespoon of flour and continuing to whisk at high speed to aerate and rescue the mixture.

Pour the whole beaten eggs from a jug in a very slow steady stream into the creamed butter and sugar, with the electric whisk on high speed. This will take up to 20 minutes. Remove the electric beater. Sift the flour into the bowl. This will remove any lumps in the flour and add more air into the cake batter as the flour aerates.

✗ What not to do

Don't beat the flour into the cake batter – this will knock out the air bubbles and activate the elasticated, stretchy gluten protein resulting in a chewy, dense-textured cake. Fold in carefully by hand with a metal blade or rubber spatula until well mixed.

Carefully fold in the flour using a metal spoon or flat-bladed spatula. This involves carefully drawing the spatula around the edge of the mixture and turning it over with a cutting action until the flour is incorporated. Carefully transfer the mixture into the prepared cake tin. Hold the bowl close to the tin so it does not have to be dolloped from a great height, which would knock out the air.

It is not possible to over-cream a cake mixture. I cream my cakes for 10 minutes on maximum speed to ensure high levels of aeration and emulsification before adding the eggs.

MICH'S TIPS

1 The butter should be taken out of the fridge and allowed to come up to room temperature naturally. Don't be tempted to soften the butter in the microwave – it will simply melt and not have the aeration properties. Cold butter will not cream and will result in a grainy, close, dense cake. It is not technically possible to over-cream the butter and sugar – the longer the better.

2 Egg white (albumen) is an elastic protein and works best when warmed up. If egg white is cold the protein will not stretch around the air bubbles – resulting in a dense cake. Eggs at room temperature will have maximum aeration. Cold eggs are more susceptible to curdling when added to a cake mixture – again resulting in a dense cake. Egg yolk contains lecithin – a good emulsifier.

3 You practically need to hold your breath while you fold in the flour with the lightest of touches to ensure the flour is incorporated, the batter is smooth and the minimum amount of air bubbles destroyed. If the flour is beaten in too heavily, the gluten will develop and the resulting cake will be tough, dry and chewy.

4 Ensure the oven is switched on to the correct temperature as you start making the cake. It is important the oven is at the right temperature for the cake so that it can be put straight in as soon as it is in the tin. Any delay in waiting for the oven to come to temperature at this stage would allow the cake batter to settle, air to be lost or raising agent to start working and lose some of its potency before baking, resulting in a dense cake.

Use the back of the spatula to smooth the surface of the cake batter in the tin. The cake is now ready to be baked. Bake in the oven for the stated time or until the cake is a golden colour and a skewer inserted in the centre comes out clean. Remove the cake from the oven and leave in the tin to cool for 10 minutes. The perfect creamed cake should have an even rise and even texture with uniform air bubbles throughout the cake. The crust will be springy and neither tough nor chewy.

"It takes time to make and bake the perfect cake. I have seen many bakers rush to get the cake in the oven, often cutting corners in the process."

Shallow sides and peaked cake

Close, dense texture

✘ What not to do

Adding all the flour and beating in with the electric whisk will incorporate the flour and help stabilize the batter. However, it will also work the gluten in the flour – encouraging it to strengthen, become more elasticated and chewy – sadly it will have this same effect on the baked cake. The resulting batter looks dense, darker and thick. The resulting cake can clearly be seen to have a poor rise on the sides of the cake and an over-risen crust in the centre. This is due to the lack of aeration during the making and allowing only for the raising agent in the flour to force the centre of the cake up as it bakes. The texture is uneven, dense and the cake looks dârker with a chewy, tough bite. Not creaming for long enough will prevent the batter from having sufficient air incorporated into the cake – the cake will be dense, tough, with lower sides and a peak in the centre.

Creamed chocolate cake

Chocolate cakes are indulgent and delectable but there is a real skill to baking the perfect chocolate cake to ensure it has the right intensity of flavour. It should be rich, neither bland nor bitter and overpowering, balanced with a moist texture and also with a soft bite. Chocolate cake should always be eaten at room temperature as chilled chooclate will make the cake feel drier than it is.

Makes a 20cm (8 inch) round cake (see also page 82 for other sizes)

INGREDIENTS

250g (8oz) unsalted butter, softened

350g (11½oz) soft brown sugar

5 medium eggs, beaten

200g (7oz) melted dark chocolate (70% cocoa solids)

1 tablespoon vanilla bean paste

140g (4½oz) plain flour

Preheat the oven to 160°C (313°F/ Gas 3).

Creaming the butter and sugar together creates an aerated emulsion. Place the butter and sugar in a clean bowl and whisk slowly at first to incorporate the two ingredients. For this chocolate cake I have suggested soft brown sugar as the molasses will ensure the resulting cake has a chewy caramelized texture. Refined or caster sugar would result in a drier, crispier cake, which would taste sweet, but not have a caramelized undertone.

Add the beaten egg in a slow steady stream, beating well to incorporate the egg into the creamed mixture.

Don't be tempted to soften butter in the microwave – it will simply melt and not have the aeration properties necessary to make a light-as-air cake.

✗ What not to do

Using cold ingredients or rushing either of the creaming or adding eggs stages will result in a curdled cake mixture. A curdled mixture has globules of slimy batter with oozing liquid. Whilst it is preferable to avoid this, it is possible to still use this mixture to make a cake. Continue to whisk in its current state for 10 minutes with the addition of a little melted chocolate (contains more lecithin – a natural stabilizer and emulsifier) or flour (the starch will soak up the liquid and stabilize the batter). The resulting cake will be dense, tight and chewy but should still have a good flavour.

Chocolate should be melted to allow even incorporation through the cake. Leave it to cool before adding to avoid melting the butter and therefore reducing aeration. Don't be tempted to use chocolate with lower cocoa solids as the cake recipe has been formulated to use these solids to help set the cake and impart a decadent chocolate flavour.

Once the chocolate is fully incorporated the resulting cake batter should have the texture of whipped chocolate mousse.

I like to add a tablespoon of vanilla bean paste at this stage. Vanilla greatly enhances the flavour of chocolate (it is added as an integral ingredient in chocolate manufacturing) by providing a pleasant aftertaste.

MICH'S TIPS

1 Before you start, ensure all ingredients are at room temperature. This will allow for maximum aeration, resulting in a light, even-textured cake.

2 Use the best, freshest quality ingredients – it sounds simple, but don't think ingredients that are past their prime will miraculously improve once baked in a cake. It is advisable to use the freshest, plumpest, tastiest, highest quality ingredients to produce spectacular cakes.

3 Melt the chocolate and leave to cool before adding to the batter so it does not melt the butter (which would reduce the aeration) or cook the eggs.

4 Measure all ingredients accurately. Making cakes is scientific. All ingredients are included for a reason and as such it is imperative the weights and measures are adhered to accurately. Too much or too little of the key ingredients will dramatically affect the result.

5 Use chocolate with a minimum 70% cocoa solids to be sure to impart a rich, indulgent chocolate flavour.

6 Adding the zest of 2 oranges or 100g chopped roasted pecans add wonderful variations to this chocolate cake recipe.

  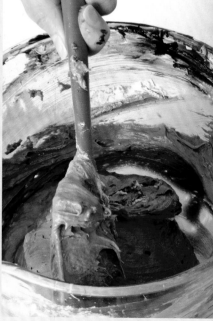

Flour is folded into the cake mixture with the lightest of touches. Beating with a heavy hand, wooden spoon or an electric mixer would knock out air incorporated during creaming and overwork the gluten (protein) in the flour. This would result in a tough, chewy, dense cake. Remove the bowl from the electric mixer and continue by hand. Tip the flour into the bowl and use a spatula or metal spoon to carefully fold (cutting and turning action) together. Practically hold your breath at this stage and stop as soon as the cake mixture is evenly mixed.

Tip the cake mixture into the prepared, lined 20cm (8in) round tin (see pages 24–25) and level with the back of the spatula. Bake in the preheated oven for 1 hour.

This chocolate cake will rise (thanks to all the aeration) and have a slight wobble as it comes out of the oven. The crust will be risen and crispy and the cake underneath will be gently glistening as it is removed from the oven – neither completely dry (overbaked) or wet (underbaked). Leave to cool in the tin. The crust will settle back down and the top edges may crack as the cake cools – this is perfectly normal.

Testing if a cake is baked

There is nothing worse than spending time perfecting cake-baking methods, to then have it ruined by over- or underbaking. These tips will ensure you bake your cakes to perfection every time. As ovens vary, make a note for each recipe as you attempt it, recording your perfect baking time for the future.

TESTING WITH A SKEWER

Use an oven cloth to carefully remove the cake from the oven and place on a wire cooling rack. Check the cake is baked by inserting a cake skewer in the centre. If the cake skewer comes out clean the cake is baked.

HOW TO TELL IF THE CAKE IS BAKED

There are several methods to ensure a cake is properly baked.

* Has the cake had the time stated in the recipe?

* Does it smell baked?

* The cake should gently come away from the sides of the tin.

* The top should be firm but spring back when pressed lightly.

* The cake should have a golden colour (although this is hard to tell if baking a chocolate cake).

* Most cakes can be checked by inserting a skewer or small knife in the centre, which should come out clean (see above).

> Get to know your oven well and trust your instincts: if you know your oven generally runs quite hot, check your cake towards the end of the bake time to ensure it doesn't over cook.

✕ What can go wrong

Simple changes to the baking environment can have a dramatic effect on the end result of a baked cake.

Plain flour

This cake has been baked for the correct time at the correct temperature but with no or old raising agent. The cake is flat and shallow with a very close crumb. It is important to ensure all the ingredients, including the raising agents, are fresh.

15 min over

This cake has been overbaked by 15 minutes at the correct temperature. You can see the top is dark with a thick crust. The cake crumb inside will be slightly dry as more moisture has been driven out of the cake by the extra baking time.

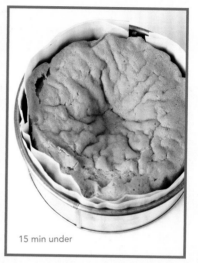

15 min under

This cake has been underbaked by 15 minutes at the correct temperature. You can see the surface is pale and the cake has collapsed in the centre. The cake has not had enough time for the starch and protein to complete their roles in stabilizing and supporting the cake.

Oven too cold

This cake has been baked for the correct length of time, but in an oven set 20 degrees cooler than stated. The result is an anaemic, cake that has sunk in the centre where it is still raw.

Oven too hot

This cake has been baked for the correct length of time, but in an oven set 20 degrees hotter than stated. It has a very thick, dark crust and is quite shallow. The protein, starch and raising agent have been forced to work too hard, too fast, not allowing for an even rise.

> *" It is essential to have the oven at the correct temperature and always bake for the stated time."*

HEAVENLY VANILLA CAKE

This cake has to be the ultimate vanilla cake to include in your armoury. It is a to-die-for cake that never fails to impress when we serve it at Little Venice Cake Company. The secret is the quality of the ingredients and emphasizing the flavour of the cake with vanilla bean paste. The result is a nostalgic vanilla cake that quite literally nurtures the soul. Food for the Gods!

☀ CREAMED METHOD

Makes a 20cm (8 inch) round cake (see also page 82 for other sizes)

INGREDIENTS

300g (10½oz) unsalted butter, softened

300g (10½oz) golden caster sugar

6 large eggs, beaten

420g (15oz) self-raising flour

6 tablespoons fresh milk

3 tablespoons vanilla bean paste

FOR THE SYRUP

150ml (¼ pint) water

115g (3¾oz) golden caster sugar

2 tablespoons vanilla bean paste

Preheat the oven to 160°C (313°F/gas 3). Line a 20cm (8 inch) round tin with non-stick baking parchment.

TO MAKE THE CAKE

Use the cake ingredients below to make your cake following the creamed cake method on pages 34–37) adding the milk and vanilla bean paste after the flour has been folded in. Bake in the preheated oven for 1½ hours.

TO MAKE THE SYRUP

Many cakes can benefit from being spiked with a delicious syrup as they are removed from the oven. This will help to keep them moist and add flavour.

Measure the water, golden caster sugar and vanilla bean paste into a saucepan. Heat gently until the sugar dissolves, stirring all the time, then remove from the heat.

Use an oven cloth to carefully remove the cake from the oven and place on a wire cooling rack. Check the cake is baked by inserting a cake skewer in the centre. If the cake skewer comes out clean the cake is baked and ready to be spiked with syrup. Use a clean metal skewer or disposable cocktail stick and pierce the cake all over, making sure you reach all the way to the bottom of the cake. This will ensure the syrup reaches the whole cake – not just the top half.

Pour or spoon the syrup slowly and evenly over the whole cake. Leave to cool in the tin to allow the cake to soak up all the syrup.

Storage: This cake will keep for 5 days and is perfect split and layered with buttercream as the base for numerous celebration cakes.

VARIATIONS

1 Lemon Cake – substitute 2 tablespoons of the vanilla bean paste with the zest of 4 lemons. For the syrup, use 150ml (¼ pint) fresh lemon juice strained through a tea strainer instead of the water and omit the vanilla bean paste. It is not necessary to heat this syrup as the acid in the lemon juice will dissolve the sugar.

2 Orange Cake – add the zest of 2 large oranges and 2 teaspoons natural orange oil to the cake. Add 2 teaspoons natural orange oil to the syrup.

3 Coffee Cake – add 1 tablespoon natural coffee essence or 2 shots cooled strong espresso (about 80ml/3¼fl oz of liquid) and reduce the milk to 3 tablespoons. For the syrup, replace 75ml (3fl oz) of the water with 1 shot of espresso.

Don't over-syrup the cake. The syrup should be absorbed within 1 minute and the top should not be soggy. Retain any extra syrup to be brushed onto the cut surface of the cakes with a pastry brush.

"Try using different sugars in the base of the tin, such as light brown sugar for a more indulgent caramel sauce."

☀ CREAMED CAKE METHOD

Makes 4 small 10cm (4 inch) cakes or 1 larger 20cm (8 inch) round cake

FOR THE TOPPING (BASE OF THE TIN)

55g (2oz) unsalted butter, melted

80g (2¾oz) demerara sugar

80g (2¾oz) golden caster sugar

1 medium fresh pineapple, peeled, cored and cut into rings about 1cm (½ inch) thick

FOR THE CAKE

115g (3¾oz) unsalted butter, softened

200g (7oz) golden caster sugar

1 tablespoon vanilla bean paste

2 large eggs, separated

195g (7oz) plain flour

2 teaspoons baking powder

120ml (4¼fl oz) semi-skimmed milk

¼ teaspoon cream of tartar

Preheat oven to 180°C (350°F/Gas 4). Line four 10cm (4 inch) round cake tins or one 20cm (8 inch) round cake tin with non-stick baking parchment.

PINEAPPLE UPSIDE-DOWN CAKE

It has been a treat to reinvent this classic cake, which just happens to be my husband's favourite of all time. Fresh pineapple takes on a wonderful golden colour and intense caramelized flavour when it is baked, which completely transforms this cake. Try using different sugars in the base of the tin, such as light brown sugar for a more indulgent caramel sauce rather than a crispy bite.

TO MAKE THE TOPPING

Melt the butter and spoon it evenly between the lined tins. Swirl each tin to evenly coat the base with the melted butter.

Mix the sugars together in a small bowl and use a spoon to sprinkle evenly over the butter between the tins.

Use a sharp knife or a 10cm (4 inch) circular cutter to press out 4 clean discs of pineapple from each 1cm (½ inch) slice. Remove the core from each cut circle with a smaller cutter or knife. Place a pineapple ring into the base of each tin. (If you are using a larger tin, position the pineapple rings over the base of the tin).

> *❝I sometimes add grated root ginger to the cake batter for an added bite.❞*

TO PREPARE THE CAKE

Cream the butter and sugar together following the instructions on page 34.

Mix the vanilla and egg yolks together in a jug and then add slowly to the bowl as you continue mixing on high speed.

Sift the flour and baking powder into the bowl. Use a metal spoon or flat-blade spatula and carefully fold in the flour. Add the milk.

Whisk the egg whites in a clean bowl with the cream of tartar until soft peaks form. Fold into the cake batter in two additions.

Carefully pour the batter between the tins and over the pineapple. Bake in the preheated oven for 40–45 minutes or until the cake is golden brown and a cake skewer inserted in the centre comes out clean.

Leave to cool for 10 minutes in the tin, then turn out onto a serving plate. Serve warm with fresh whipped cream or vanilla custard.

Storage: Best eaten on the day of making.

COURGETTE PECAN LOAF

Incorporating vegetables into cakes adds moistness as well as nutrition, flavour, texture and colour. This loaf cake is deliciously moist, nutty and flavourful with a cinnamon spiced note added with juicy sultanas. Good for breakfast I say!

✳ CREAMED CAKE METHOD

Makes a 1kg (2¼ lb) loaf

INGREDIENTS

200g (7oz) unsalted butter, softened

200g (7oz) golden caster sugar

2 medium eggs

215g (7½oz) courgettes

200g (7oz) plain flour

Large pinch of sea salt

½ teaspoon baking powder

1 teaspoon ground cinnamon

60g (2oz) chopped pecans

80g (3oz) sultanas

20g (¾oz) demerara sugar

Preheat the oven to 180°C (350°F/Gas 4). Butter and line the base and sides of a 1kg (2¼ lb) loaf tin with non-stick baking parchment.

Cream the butter and sugar together following the instructions on page 34.

Beat the eggs together in a jug, then add slowly to the bowl as you continue mixing on high speed until stable and aerated.

Grate the courgettes. Squeeze them with your hands to remove any excess moisture, then add to the creamed mixture. It is essential to squeeze the courgettes to remove the excess moisture and concentrate the flavour. If all this moisture were left in the cake, it would be too soggy.

In a separate bowl, sift together the flour, salt, baking powder and cinnamon, then gently fold this into the creamed mixture. Stir in the pecans and sultanas.

Spoon the batter into the prepared loaf tin and sprinkle the surface with demerara sugar.

Bake in the preheated oven for 1 hour or until the cake is golden brown and firm to the touch.

Leave to cool in the tin on a wire rack before turning out onto the wire rack. Serve in thick slices cut with a serrated knife.

Storage: Keeps for 7 days in an airtight container, wrapped in greaseproof paper.

Note: To ensure the sultanas are succulent, soak them in orange juice for 1–2 hours to plump up before baking.

> *It is essential to squeeze the courgettes to remove the excess moisture and concentrate the flavour.*

2 The Whisked Cake Method

Whisked cakes are super light and airy. They have very little, if any, fat and are often accompanied by cream- or butter-based fillings to add flavour and mouthfeel. Due to their low-fat content they don't keep well and should be eaten within 2 days to be at their best. Many roulades are made with this method so the cakes are visually interesting and make wonderful centrepieces for a special occasion.

Makes a 23cm (9 inch) round cake

INGREDIENTS

4 medium eggs

125g (4½oz) golden caster sugar

25g (1oz) unsalted butter, melted

125g (4½oz) plain four

Preheat the oven to 180°C (350°F/Gas 4). Base-line a 23cm (9 inch) springform non-stick tin with non-stick baking parchment.

Place the eggs and sugar in a large glass bowl set over a saucepan filled with a 2.5cm (1 inch) depth of water. Turn the heat to moderate until the water is simmering nicely. Whisk with a hand-held electric whisk as the mixture is warmed from underneath and continue to whip on high speed for about 10 minutes, until the mixture is aerated, pale and voluminous.

The heat will enhance the whisking process – warming and stabilizing the eggs during aeration. The mixture should be soft and pillowy and leave a 'ribbon trail' when it is fully aerated.

This method involves whisking together the eggs and sugar over very gentle heat, then folding in the melted butter and flour before baking.

"Whisking the eggs and sugar together over a heat creates a sabayon."

✖ What not to do

If the eggs and sugar are not sufficiently whisked to the ribbon stage, the mixture cannot support the butter and flour in a suspended mallowy cake batter. The mixture is very runny and has to be poured into the tin. The resulting cake will be dense and sticky. It is unlikely to bake and handle properly – lacking the air to give it a spongy texture.

Drizzle the melted butter around the outer edge of the bowl to prevent knocking out the air bubbles. Sift the flour over the surface of the batter to remove any lumps and add extra aeration. Use a metal spoon or flat-blade spatula to gently fold the butter and flour into the whisked mixture until it is fully incorporated, glossy and velvet. The mixture is now ready to transfer to the prepared baking tin. Bake in the preheated oven for 25–30 minutes.

COFFEE HAZELNUT ROULADE

with salted caramel and crunchy praline

This is a particularly adult cake – combining espresso with roasted hazelnuts and a homemade crunchy caramelized praline. The textures and flavours are indulgent so serve this cake with espresso for a delectable treat.

☀ WHISKED CAKE METHOD

Makes a 23cm (9 inch) Swiss roll (serves 8)

FOR THE ROULADE

4 large eggs

110g (3¾oz) golden caster sugar, plus extra for sprinkling

55g (2oz) unsalted butter, melted and cooled

1 shot (2½ tablespoons) espresso, cooled – alternatively, dissolve 2 teaspoons coffee essence in 40ml (2½ tablespoons) water

115g (3¾oz) plain flour

50g (1¾oz) roasted hazelnuts, chopped (see Tip)

FOR THE FILLING

½ quantity Buttercream (see page 104), made with unrefined icing sugar

3 tablespoons Salted Caramel (see page 92)

3 tablespoons crushed Praline (see page 96), plus extra to decorate

Preheat the oven to 190°C (375°F/Gas 5). Line a 22.5 x 33cm (9 x 11 inch) Swiss roll tin with non-stick baking parchment.

TO MAKE THE ROULADE

Use the eggs, sugar, butter, espresso and flour to make the cake batter following the whisked cake method on pages 50–51.

Pour into the prepared Swiss roll tin, levelling the batter into the corners with the back of a spoon. Sprinkle the surface with the chopped roasted hazelnuts.

Bake in the preheated oven for 15–20 minutes until the cake is well risen and the surface springs back when lightly pressed.

Place a sheet of non-stick baking parchment on top of a clean damp tea towel on a work surface and lightly sprinkle the parchment with caster sugar.

As soon as the cake is baked, remove it from the oven and upturn it onto the parchment. Peel the paper away in strips, being careful to protect the surface of the roulade. See page 31 for further instructions.

"I sometimes use mascarpone instead of the buttercream for a less sweet version."

TO ROLL THE ROULADE

Roll the roulade up from the short edge, keeping the non-stick baking parchment inside the roll. Wrap the roulade in the clean, damp tea towel and leave to cool.

Unravel the roulade and spread the entire surface with buttercream.

Fill a small piping bag with the salted caramel, snip the end with a sharp pair of scissors and drizzle the salted caramel over the surface of the buttercream. Scatter the crushed praline over the top.

Roll the roulade up from the short end, discarding the baking parchment. Transfer to a serving plate and decorate with additional praline.

Storage: Store any leftover roulade in the fridge for up to 24 hours, but remove from the fridge 30 minutes before serving to allow the flavours to develop.

To roast the hazelnuts, place them on a heavy baking tray and roast in an oven preheated to 190°C (375°F/Gas 5) for 10–12 minutes. Transfer to a clean tea towel and rub the nuts to remove the skins. Leave to cool.

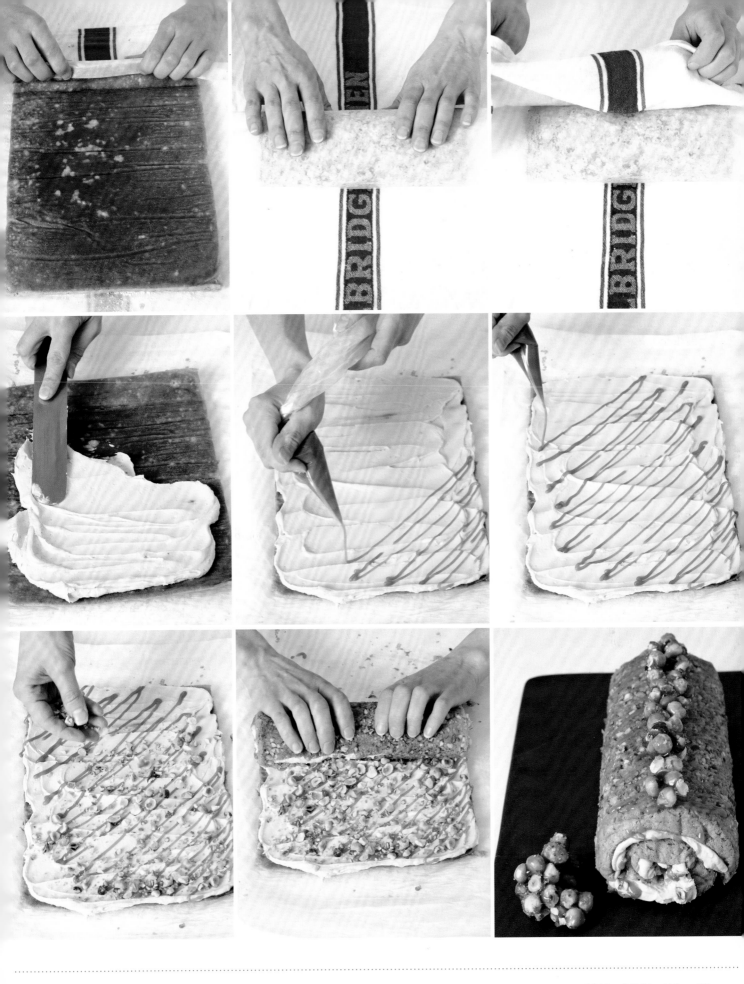

CHOCOLATE CHERRY GENOISE

This cake combines a classic combination of light chocolate roulade with fresh whipped cream and kirsch-soaked morello cherries. Roulades look impressive but are very simple to make. I have chosen to decorate this cake with gilded fresh cherries and hand-piped leaves of fresh cream – after all, 'life is just a bowl of cherries.'

☀ WHISKED CAKE METHOD

Makes a 23cm (9 inch)
Swiss roll (serves 8)

INGREDIENTS

4 large eggs

110g (3¾ oz) golden caster sugar

55g (2oz) unsalted butter, melted and cooled

85g (3oz) plain flour

30g (1¼oz) cocoa powder, plus 1 tablespoon for dusting

1 x 390g (13½oz) jar morello cherries (250g/9oz drained weight)

2 tablespoons kirsch

300ml (½ pint) double cream

6–8 fresh cherries

3 sheets edible gold leaf

Preheat the oven to 190°C (375°F/Gas 5). Line a 22.5 x 33cm (9 x 11 inch) Swiss roll tin with non-stick baking parchment.

TO MAKE THE ROULADE

Use the eggs, sugar, butter, flour and cocoa powder to make the cake batter following the whisked cake method on pages 50–51.

Pour into the prepared Swiss roll tin, levelling the batter into the corners with the back of a spoon. Bake for 15–20 minutes until the cake is well risen and the surface springs back when lightly pressed.

Place a sheet of non-stick baking parchment on top of a clean damp tea towel on a work surface and lightly dust the parchment with cocoa powder.

As soon as the cake is baked, remove it from the oven and upturn it onto the dusted parchment. Peel the paper away in strips (see page 31). Roll the roulade up from the short edge, keeping the non-stick baking parchment inside the roll. Wrap the roulade in the clean, damp tea towel and leave to cool.

Drain the cherries into a bowl, pour over the kirsch and leave to infuse.

TO ROLL THE ROULADE

When you are ready to fill the roulade, whip the cream. Spoon 3 tablespoons of the whipped cream into a large piping bag fitted with a leaf (No. 69) nozzle and set aside.

Unroll the roulade and spread the rest of the whipped cream over the entire surface. Scatter with the morello cherries, then roll up and transfer to a serving plate.

Use a paintbrush to dampen the surface of the fresh cherries with water, then press gold leaf onto the cherries with a clean paintbrush.

Pipe a row of cream leaves along the length of the roulade, then decorate with the gilded fresh cherries to finish.

This cake should be served and eaten within 4 hours.

Storage: Store any leftover roulade in the fridge for up to 24 hours, but remove from the fridge 30 minutes before serving to allow the flavours to develop.

Use as many or as few cherries inside the roulade as you like. Blitz the remainder with a hand-held blender, adding 1 tablespoon kirsch and enough drained juice to make a purée to accompany the roulade.

Makes a 20cm (8 inch)
round cake

INGREDIENTS

3 navel oranges (about
280g/9¾oz in total),
scrubbed – 2 roughly
chopped and 1 for
fresh zest

5 medium eggs,
separated

200g (7oz) golden caster
sugar

225g (8oz) ground
almonds

1 teaspoon natural orange
oil

TO COVER

½ quantity Dark Chocolate
Ganache (see pages
100–101) with 1
tablespoon natural
orange oil added

2 tablespoons sieved
apricot jam, heated

300g (10½oz) almond
marzipan (minimum
35% ground almonds)

Edible gold lustre, to finish

Preheat the oven to 180°C
(350°F/Gas 4). Line a
20cm (8 inch) round
cake tin with non-stick
baking parchment.

ORANGE & ALMOND CAKE

This gluten-free cake has a wonderfully rich Seville orange marmalade flavour, which is why I have chosen to cover the cake with a layer of almond marzipan and chocolate orange ganache.

Put the chopped oranges (minus pips, but with peel) in a saucepan. Add 1 tablespoon water, cover and simmer for 30 minutes until soft and all the water has been absorbed. Leave to cool. Blend the entire oranges in a food processor or with a hand-held blender to form a smooth thick paste.

In a separate bowl, whisk the egg yolks with half the sugar until pale and thick. Carefully whisk in the orange paste and fold in the ground almonds. Stir in the orange oil and zest.

Put the egg whites in a large clean bowl and whisk until soft peaks form. Gradually whisk in the remaining sugar, a teaspoon at a time, on high speed until you have a glossy meringue. Stir 2 tablespoons of meringue into the cake batter to slacken the mixture, then fold in the remaining meringue until well incorporated.

Pour the batter into the tin and bake for 50 minutes until a skewer inserted in the centre comes out clean. Check after 20 minutes and cover with baking parchment or aluminium foil if it is browning too much. Leave the cake to cool in the tin before turning out.

Turn the cake upside down and place on a 20cm (8 inch) cake board. Skim coat the

top and sides with half the dark chocolate orange ganache using a palette knife (see page 107). The ganache should be a spreading consistency. Place the cake in the freezer for 10 minutes to firm, while you heat the jam in a small pan.

Remove the cake from the freezer and brush with apricot jam. Knead and roll the marzipan to a circle large enough to cover the top and sides of the cake (see pages 136–143). The marzipan should be about 3mm thick. Trim and smooth with icing smoothers once the marzipan is in place.

Place the cake on a wire rack and heat the remaining chocolate orange ganache until it is pouring consistency. Use a ladle to spoon the ganache over the top of the cake and swirl it around the top and sides (see page 111). Tap the wire rack to remove any excess ganache. Lift the cake and remove any excess trimmings from the base of the cake board. Take a 10cm (4 inch) crank-handled palette knife and smooth the ganache up and down around the sides of the cake. Spray with gold lustre before placing on a pretty cake stand to serve.

Storage: Store in an airtight container in a cool, dry place and consume within 3 days.

3 The Batter & Foam Method

Cakes made with oil rather than butter can be chilled successfully, while still retaining their moistness. Butter or hard fats in a cake will harden and solidify in the fridge, which can cause them to taste dry. These batter and foam cakes are super light but due to their reasonable amount of liquid fat will have better keeping properties than a whisked cake. The flavour of the base cake tends to be quite bland and carries additional flavourings such as orange and lemon very well. Batter and foam cakes can support the addition of fresh fruit and creams, which also require refrigeration. The method involves stirring and folding a meringue foam into a cake batter.

TO MAKE THE BATTER

Makes a 23cm (9 inch) cake (serves 16)

INGREDIENTS

7 large egg yolks, separated, plus 2 large egg whites

120ml (4¼fl oz) sunflower oil

180ml (6fl oz) full-fat milk

270g (9¾oz) plain flour

2¼ teaspoons baking powder

300g (10½oz) granulated sugar

½ teaspoon cream of tartar

Preheat the oven to 170°C (325°F/Gas 3). You will need a 23cm/1.8 litre (9 inch/ 3 pint) ring mould, unlined.

Place the egg yolks, oil and milk into the clean bowl of a kitchen mixer. Beat the liquid ingredients on moderate speed for about 3 minutes until smooth. In a separate bowl, mix together the flour, baking powder and sugar. Tip these into the eggs and oil. Beat the ingredients together until they are well combined, smooth and no lumps remain.

TO MAKE THE FOAM

As the foam begins to stablize you could also add vanilla bean paste for added flavour or any other flavouring you like (flavoured oils, coffee etc.)

Place the reserved egg whites in a separate bowl, making sure the bowl is super clean and dry and the egg whites are at room temperature. Whisk the egg whites until just foaming, then add the cream of tartar to strengthen the foam. As the foam begins to stabilize, add vanilla bean paste or other flavouring.

"It is imperative that the tin is not lined so the cake will rise beautifully and literally crawl up the sides of the tin."

Once the egg white foam reaches the firm peak stage add the sugar a tablespoon at a time, whisking well between each addition. This will ensure the sugar is evenly distributed and the meringue is stable and glossy. The foam is ready when it is super thick, voluminous and glossy with the sugar fully incorporated.

MICH'S TIPS

1 This recipe differs from an Angel Food Cake, which is made with egg white, sugar and flour and has no fat at all, but the principle of an unlined tube pan is the same – to allow the cake batter to rise and cling to the sides of the tin as it bakes.

2 It is really important to allow the cake to cool upside down in the tin, suspended over a bowl or similar, to allow the steam to escape so the cakes does not become soggy or collapse down on itself.

MIXING THE BATTER & FOAM

Stir one third of the foam into the batter with a spoon to slacken the mixture. Add the second third of the foam and use a combination of stirring and folding to incorporate the foam into the batter. Add the final third of the foam and fold carefully with a flat-blade spatula. The cake mixture will be ready to transfer to the tin when it is silky smooth, voluminous and no lumps of foam remain. Bake in the preheated oven for 50 minutes.

"Make sure the bowl is scrupulously clean before whisking the egg whites. Any grease will inhibit the eggs reaching their full aeration."

Makes a 25cm (10 inch)
round cake

INGREDIENTS

175g (6oz) plain flour

50g (1¾oz) polenta

300g (10½oz) golden
caster sugar

1 tablespoon baking
powder

2 tablespoons freshly
grated orange zest

6 large eggs, separated,
plus 1 large egg white

½ teaspoon cream of
tartar

120ml (4fl oz) sunflower oil
(or canola or corn oil)

180ml (6fl oz) freshly
squeezed orange juice,
strained

2 teaspoons vanilla bean
paste

1 teaspoon natural orange
oil

Vanilla sugar, to finish

Fresh berries, to serve

Preheat the oven to
170°C (325°F/Gas 3).
You will also need a
25cm (10 inch) tube
pan, ungreased.

ORANGE CHIFFON CAKE

This cake is all about the orange and is delicate, moist, melt-in-the-mouth, light, fluffy and full of flavour. Serve with fresh summer fruits and ice cream or sorbet. It keeps very well and can be refrigerated.

Place the flour, polenta, 250g (9oz) of the sugar, the baking powder and orange zest in a large bowl and beat until combined.

Make a well in the centre and add the egg yolks, oil, orange juice, vanilla bean paste and orange oil. Beat until you have a smooth batter.

In a separate bowl, whisk the egg whites until just foaming. Add the cream of tartar and continue to whisk until soft peaks form.

Add the remaining sugar a teaspoon at a time while continuing to whisk until the sugar is fully incorporated and the meringue is glossy and stiff. Fold the egg white foam into the batter in three additions until fully incorporated.

Pour into the tube pan or ring mould and bake for 55 minutes or until risen, golden

brown and a cake skewer inserted into the centre comes out clean.

Place an upturned glass bowl on the work surface. Invert the cake in the tin onto the glass bowl and leave to cool.

Run a palette knife around the outside and inside and carefully remove the cake. Place on a cake stand and dredge heavily with vanilla dusting sugar. Serve with fresh summer berries.

Storage: This cake keeps extremely well stored in the refrigerator for up to 5 days without drying out.

Vanilla sugar: To make your own decant a box of icing sugar into a large storage jar. Split a vanilla pod with a sharp knife and place the pod inside the jar. Seal the jar to allow the sugar to take on the vanilla flavour.

✗ What not to do

Ensure egg whites are fully whisked to create a stable foam. Adding egg whites before this stage will result in a dense, shallow cake.

BEETROOT CAKE

I love the jewel tones in this cake when it is cut open – a rich beetroot colour speckled with golden sultanas and cranberries, packed full of flavour with roasted, chopped hazelnuts and spices. This cake goes particularly well with morning coffee or afternoon tea – it is what I would call an 'anytime cake'.

✳ BATTER & FOAM METHOD

Makes a 23cm (9 inch) round ring mould cake

INGREDIENTS

200ml (7fl oz) groundnut oil

250g (9oz) golden caster sugar

3 medium eggs, separated

3 tablespoons milk

150g (5½oz) raw beetroot, peeled and grated

100g (3½oz) roasted hazelnuts, chopped (see page 52)

100g (3½oz) golden sultana and dried cranberry mix

200g (7oz) plain flour

2 teaspoons baking powder

½ teaspoon ground ginger

1 teaspoon ground cinnamon

1 teaspoon freshly grated nutmeg

½ teaspoon cream of tartar

Preheat the oven to 190°C (375°F/Gas 5). Liberally spray a ring mould with non-stick spray (see page 26).

Whisk together the oil and sugar in a large bowl until combined. Add the egg yolks and milk and continue to whisk until you have a smooth batter. Stir in the grated beetroot, nuts and vine fruits.

In a separate bowl, mix together the flour, baking powder and spices. Stir into the beetroot cake batter.

Place the egg whites in a clean bowl and whisk until just foaming. Add the cream of tartar and continue to whisk on full speed until they reach the stiff peak stage.

Fold the egg white foam into the batter in three stages until smooth and well combined.

Transfer the cake mixture to the prepared tin and bake for 30–35 minutes or until a skewer inserted in the centre comes out clean.

Remove from the oven and place on a wire rack to cool. Run a knife around the edge of the cake before turning out onto a serving plate or cake stand.

Storage: This cake stores well wrapped in greaseproof paper and tin foil in the fridge for up to 7 days.

Beetroot is a good source of folates and nitrates, which can help reduce blood pressure. It has a wonderful earthy taste and adds a rich colour.

4 The All-in-one Method

The all-in-one method involves measuring all ingredients into a bowl and beating with an electric whisk for 10 minutes until smooth and combined. There are no separate stages of creaming, adding egg and folding in the flour to incorporate air so extra raising agent is added to ensure the cake will rise. Milk may be added to provide extra moistness. It is imperative all ingredients are at room temperature and although softer margarine can be used instead of butter, the taste will be compromised. All-in-one method cakes are great for novice bakers or those particularly short of time.

Place the accurately measured ingredients in the clean bowl of a kitchen mixer. Make sure the raising agent is fresh to ensure potency. Turn the mixer on slow speed at first to combine the ingredients, then on full speed for 10 minutes. The cake batter will be ready when it is light and pale. The volume will have increased but not as much as for a creamed cake. Add more milk as necessary to ensure the cake batter will drop off a spoon with a sharp tap. Pour into the prepared cake tin and bake in the preheated oven for 1 hour.

Makes a 15cm (6 inch) round cake

INGREDIENTS

175g (6oz) unsalted butter

175g (6oz) golden caster sugar

3 large eggs

175g (6oz) plain flour

2 tablespoons milk

2 teaspoons baking powder

2 teaspoons vanilla extract

Preheat the oven to 160°C (313°F/ Gas 3). Line a 15cm (6 inch) round tin with non-stick baking parchment.

MICH'S TIPS

1 Make sure all the ingredients are at room temperature and are the freshest quality.

2 Measure the raising agent accurately as the cake will rely on this for aeration.

3 Add vanilla bean paste, citrus zests, coffee, cocoa or toasted nuts to the recipe to add flavour, moisture and texture.

4 Compensate for the texture of this cake being slightly more dense by splitting the baked cake and filling with luscious homemade berry jam and either freshly whipped Crème Chantilly (see page 93) or Vanilla Buttercream (see page 104).

✘ What not to do

Under mixing the cake mixture will prevent the raising agent being evenly distributed throughout the cake. This can cause the cake to rise unevenly. Insufficient or poor quality raising agent will prevent the cake from rising evenly. Beating the flour into the cake will work the gluten, encouraging it to become more stretchy and elastic. This will make the cake more tough and chewy than a creamed cake with a denser crust.

MARBLE CAKE

I have split this recipe to make half vanilla and half chocolate. Marble cake is a perennial favourite in our house. The swirls of light and dark make the cake interesting, covered here with a sweet coffee glacé icing. This all-in-one method cake can be scaled up for larger cakes and used in shaped tins for themed birthday cakes.

☀ ALL-IN-ONE METHOD

Makes a 15cm (6 inch) round cake

INGREDIENTS

115g (3¾oz) unsalted butter, softened

115g (3¾oz) golden caster sugar

2 large eggs

115g (3¾oz) self-raising flour

1 teaspoon baking powder

40ml (2½ tablespoons) milk

1 tablespoon vanilla bean paste

20g (¾oz) cocoa powder

1 quantity Coffee Glacé Icing (see page 118)

40g (1½oz) roasted hazelnuts, chopped (see page 52), to decorate

Preheat the oven to 180°C (350°F/Gas 4). Liberally spray a 15cm (6 inch) kugelhopf tin with non-stick spray (see page 26).

Place the softened butter, sugar, eggs, flour and baking powder in a bowl with 2 tablespoons of the milk. Beat slowly at first, then on high speed for 10 minutes until fully mixed.

Divide the mixture between 2 bowls. Stir the vanilla bean paste into one of the bowls until smooth and even.

Stir the remaining milk into the cocoa powder to form a paste, add this paste to the second bowl and stir until smooth and fully incorporated.

Drop alternate spoonfuls of vanilla and chocolate cake mixture into the prepared tin until it is full.

Use a cake skewer or knife to swirl the mixture around the tin to create an interesting marble pattern, being careful not to over-mix.

Bake in the preheated oven for 45–50 minutes or until risen, golden and a skewer inserted in the centre comes out clean.

Transfer to a wire rack and leave to cool in the tin for 10 minutes before turning out.

Once cool, place on a pretty cake plate and drizzle with Coffee Glacé Icing. Decorate with roasted chopped hazelnuts.

Storage: Store in an airtight container at room temperature and consume within 2 days.

Variation: Alternatively, you could bake in 2 separate sandwich tins – one vanilla and one chocolate. Cut out rings from each cake, then sandwich them back together with buttercream or chocolate hazelnut spread to create a chequerboard-style cake.

COCONUT CAKE

This is a wonderfully creamy cake infused with coconut – it's one of my personal favourites. It keeps well and can be enjoyed with the addition of lime curd or lime buttercream. I have chosen to decorate this cake with fresh coconut shavings. Coconuts can be hard to find, and labour-intensive to shave! As an alternative, toast desiccated coconut and sprinkle over the top and sides of the cake.

☀ ALL-IN-ONE METHOD

Makes a 15cm (6 inch) round cake

INGREDIENTS

175g (6oz) unsalted butter, softened

175g (6oz) golden caster sugar

175g (6oz) self-raising flour

1½ teaspoons baking powder

3 large eggs

2 tablespoons melted creamed coconut

TO DECORATE

1 quantity Coconut Cream Frosting (see page 93)

Fresh coconut shavings, to decorate

Preheat the oven to 180°C (350°F/Gas 4). Line a 15cm (6 inch) round deep cake tin with non-stick baking parchment.

Measure all the ingredients, except the coconut, into a large bowl and mix for about 5 minutes with an electric whisk until smooth. Stir in the creamed coconut.

Pour the mixture into the prepared tin and bake in the preheated oven for 50 minutes or until a skewer inserted in the centre comes out clean.

Transfer to a wire rack and leave to cool in the tin for 10 minutes before turning out.

Place the cake on a serving plate. Spread the Coconut Cream Frosting over the top and sides of the cake with a palette knife and press the coconut shavings into the frosting to decorate.

Storage: Store in an airtight container at room temperature and consume within 3 days.

> ❝ *Coconut will add significant fat content to this cake, helping to keep it moist.* ❞

MICH'S TIPS

1 Add the grated zest of 2 limes to the cake batter for a zingy lime and coconut variation. Make a syrup with the juice from the limes mixed with 2 tablespoons golden caster sugar and stir until dissolved. Spike the cake with a skewer all over as soon as it is baked and spoon over the syrup.

2 Coconut is rich in vitamin B5, iron and zinc. It has a distinctive flavour and can be used as the hero in all areas of this cake.

5 The Melted Method

This method involves combining a liquid fat (melted butter or oil) with sugar and then beating in eggs to create a batter. Dry ingredients are stirred in and then the cake is embellished with added ingredients such as dried or fresh fruits, vegetables, nuts, spices and zest.

INGREDIENTS

See Treacle Gingerbread opposite for specific ingredients. As long as the ingredients are weighed accurately and are fresh or the best quality and the cake is baked at the right temperature for the right time, results are guaranteed.

Cakes made by the melted method are perfect for beginners to guarantee results and a moist cake, as they do not rely on any physical aeration.

Place the butter, sugar and treacle in a heavy-based saucepan over a moderate heat. Stir until completely melted, then remove from the heat and leave to cool. Stir in the beaten eggs. Mix together the flours, oatmeal and spices and stir this into the melted mixture to make a stiff batter.

Warm the milk until tepid, pour over the bicarbonate of soda in a small bowl, then add to the mixture. Pour into a prepared tin and bake in the oven for 1 hour. Leave to cool in the tin before removing and cutting into squares.

TREACLE GINGERBREAD

Don't be fooled by the unassuming innocence of these small cakes. They pack a serious punch. Laden with rich, dark sugars and syrups, they have a delicious intensity and depth combined with the potency of the stem ginger and spices. The oatmeal adds a welcome change of texture and grittiness to these cakes so they are satisfying and moreish.

☀ MELTED METHOD

Makes 40 bite-sized squares

INGREDIENTS

225g (8oz) unsalted butter

225g (8oz) soft brown sugar

225g (8oz) black treacle

2 large eggs, beaten

200g (7oz) plain flour

120g (4½oz) wholemeal flour

40g (1½oz) coarse oatmeal

2 teaspoons ground ginger

2 tablespoons chopped stem ginger

1 tablespoon ground cinnamon

290ml (9¾fl oz) milk

2 teaspoons bicarbonate of soda

Preheat the oven to 150°C (300°F/Gas 2). Line a 20 x 30cm (8 x 12 inch) loose-bottomed tin with non-stick baking parchment.

Use the ingredients above to make the gingerbread cake batter following the instructions opposite.

Pour the mixture into the prepared tin and bake in the preheated oven for 1 hour. Leave to cool in the tin before removing and cutting into squares.

Storage: This cake improves with keeping and should be stored in an airtight container at room temperature and consumed within 7 days.

MICH'S TIPS

1 Transferring the batter to a clean bowl before adding the eggs will help to cool the mixture faster. Also, place a sheet of greaseproof paper over the gingerbread after 45 minutes if it is looking too dark.

2 For a truly authentic ginger flavour, replace the ground ginger with 1–2 teaspoons fresh grated root ginger added to the batter. Taste and add more until you have the desired intensity.

Makes a 20cm (8 inch) round cake
(see also page 83 for other sizes)

FOR THE CAKE

195g (7oz) naturally coloured glacé
cherries

195g (7oz) sultanas

270g (9¾oz) raisins

330g (11½oz) currants

80g (3oz) ready-to-eat prunes, cut into
quarters

80g (3oz) Medjool dates, pitted and
cut into quarters

80g (3oz) unsulphured apricots, cut
into quarters

80g (3oz) ready-to-eat Lerida figs, cut
into quarters

175ml (6fl oz) brandy

Grated zest of 1 lemon

Grated zest of 1 orange

195g (7oz) unsalted butter

200g (7oz) dark muscovado sugar

1 tablespoon black treacle

4 eggs (medium-large), beaten

½ teaspoon vanilla extract

185g (7½oz) plain flour

½ teaspoon each of ground cinnamon,
ground ginger, ground nutmeg and
mixed spice

½ teaspoon baking powder

80g (3oz) roasted hazelnuts, chopped

30g (1oz) stem ginger

FOR THE MARZIPAN & TOPPING

200g (7oz) marzipan

110g (4oz) brazils (about 35)

110g (4oz) naturally coloured glacé
cherries (about 25)

25g (1oz) pecans (about 15)

10g (½oz) hazelnuts (about 10)

3 tablespoons apricot jam

3 tablespoons brandy

Preheat the oven to 140°C (275°F/Gas
1). Line a 20cm (8 inch) round cake
tin with a double layer of non-stick
baking parchment.

LUXURY FRUIT CAKE

A good fruit cake recipe should be the backbone of any cake-maker's repertoire. This cake keeps indefinitely if wrapped and stored well and can be made in any shape or size. It is the perfect base for any celebration cake to be covered with marzipan and icing or decorated with glazed fruits and nuts.

Weigh the cherries, vine fruits and chopped luxury fruits into a large bowl or sealable container and pour over the brandy and citrus zests. Stir well, cover and leave to steep for at least 24 hours, up to 72 hours.

Melt the butter, sugar and treacle together in a heavy-based saucepan. Remove from the heat and leave to cool slightly before adding the beaten eggs and vanilla extract; mix well.

In a separate bowl, sift together the flour, spices and baking powder and stir into the sugar batter. Mix well. Stir the steeped fruits and any remaining syrup (unlikely) into the batter together with the hazelnuts and stem ginger. Mix well.

Spoon half the cake batter into the tin and lay a disc of marzipan, cut to shape, about 4mm thick on top of the batter.

Spoon the remaining batter on the top and level the surface with the back of a spoon. Arrange rings or rows of nuts and cherries on the top before baking for 2½ hours, or until a skewer inserted into the centre comes out clean. Transfer the tin to a wire cooling rack.

Meanwhile, make an apricot brandy glaze. Put the apricot jam and brandy in a small saucepan. Heat until dissolved, smooth and just beginning to boil. Brush the surface of the cake with an apricot brandy glaze as soon as it comes out of the oven. The glaze should be warm and the cake should be hot.

Leave the cake to cool completely before turning out of the tin.

Storage: Wrap in greaseproof paper and tin foil and store at room temperature for up to 6 months.

MICH'S TIPS

1 Batch bake several fruit cakes at a time to make best use of time and ingredients.

2 Wrap the fruit cakes in a double layer of greaseproof paper and a double layer of tin foil to mature for up to 8 weeks.

3 Freshly baked fruit cakes will be crumbly. Allow the cakes to mature and the fruits to amalgamate to slice evenly and beautifully.

Makes a 23cm (9 inch)
round ring mould cake

INGREDIENTS

250ml (8½fl oz) Guinness
or stout beer

250g (9oz) unsalted butter

75g (2¾oz) cocoa powder,
plus extra for dusting

400g (14oz) golden caster
sugar

1 x 142ml (5fl oz) carton
soured cream

2 medium eggs

2 teaspoons vanilla extract

275g (9½oz) plain flour

2½ teaspoons bicarbonate
of soda

100g (3½oz) dark
chocolate chips

30g (1¼oz) oatmeal

1 quantity Cream Cheese
Frosting (see page 93)

Preheat the oven to
180°C (350°F/Gas 4).
Liberally spray a 23cm
(9 inch) ring mould with
non-stick spray (see
page 26).

CHOCOLATE BEER CAKE

This cake is made with stout, cocoa powder and soured cream to create a moist cake with a more subtle chocolate flavour than one using real melted chocolate. It has an open texture and a slightly bitter flavour that makes the cake less sweet.

Measure the stout beer into a heavy-based saucepan and add the butter. Heat over a moderate heat until the butter has melted. Whisk in the cocoa powder and the sugar, then remove from the heat.

In a separate bowl, beat together the soured cream with the eggs and vanilla extract, then pour into the beer batter.

Sift together the flour and bicarbonate of soda, then whisk it into the batter. Stir in the chocolate chips and the oatmeal. Pour the batter into the prepared tin and bake for 45–60 minutes or until the cake is well risen and a skewer inserted into the centre comes out clean.

Transfer to a wire cooling rack and leave the cake to cool completely in the tin before turning out onto a serving plate. Use a palette knife to spread over the Cream Cheese Frosting. Dust the surface with cocoa powder and cut into thick wedges to serve.

Storage: Store in an airtight container without the frosting for up to 3 days. Once frosted, best eaten on the day or stored overnight in the fridge and eaten within 48 hours (allow to come to room temperature before eating).

MICH'S TIP

Stout is a good source of iron and B vitamins. The characteristic bitter taste marries well with the cocoa and is balanced by the cream cheese frosting. To sweeten this cake add cherries, white chocolate chips or roasted nuts to the batter before it is baked. Add the zest of an orange to the cream cheese frosting for a zesty kick.

SWEET POTATO CAKE

Earthy, wholesome, dense, this cake has a delicate flavour of sweet potato combined with spices for a delicious cake. I have chosen to smother the cake in a caramel buttercream, drizzled with toffee brandy sauce and decorated with chopped crystallized ginger. But it is just as delicious without the frosting for the more health-conscious.

Makes a 23cm (9 inch) ring mould cake

INGREDIENTS

850g (1lb 12oz) red-skinned sweet potatoes

400g (14oz) light brown sugar

225ml (8fl oz) sunflower oil

4 large eggs

290g (10oz) plain flour

1 teaspoon baking powder

1 teaspoon bicarbonate of soda

½ teaspoon salt

4 teaspoons ground cinnamon

3 teaspoons ground ginger

1 teaspoon vanilla extract

1 quantity Toffee Sauce (see page 92)

1 quantity Buttercream (see page 104), but reduce the vanilla bean paste to 1 tablespoon

75g (2¾oz) crystallized stem ginger, chopped

Preheat the oven to 160°C (313°F/Gas 2–3). Spray a ring mould with non-stick baking spray (see page 26).

Place the potatoes in a baking dish and bake in the oven for 45–60 minutes, depending on their size, until tender (a knife should insert easily through the potato when it is cooked). Remove the potatoes from the oven and leave to cool before peeling and mashing the sweet potato flesh.

Place the sweet potato flesh in a large bowl and add the sugar and oil. Use an electric hand-held whisk to beat until smooth. Add the eggs a little at a time, beating well after each addition.

In a separate bowl, sift together the flour, raising agents, salt and spices. Stir into the wet ingredients and mix until just combined but no lumps remain. Stir in the vanilla.

Transfer the cake batter to the prepared tin and bake for 60–65 minutes or until a skewer inserted in the centre comes out clean.

Transfer the cake to a wire cooling rack. Run a small knife around the edge of the cake tin and leave to cool for 15 minutes before turning out and leaving to cool completely.

Transfer the cooled cake to a serving plate or cake stand.

Stir 4 tablespoons of the toffee sauce into the buttercream in a bowl. Spread the toffee buttercream over the top and sides of the cake with a palette knife.

Decorate around the base of the cake with the crystallised ginger and drizzle the remaining toffee sauce over the cake.

Storage: Keep in an airtight container at room temperature and eat within 3 days.

MICH'S TIP

Many ingredients can be added to a base batter of fat, sugar, flour and eggs to create well-flavoured cakes with interesting textures for all occasions. Root vegetables, citrus fruits, vine fruits, nuts, fresh spices and chocolate are all ingredients that can be added to cake batters.

BANANA & PECAN CAKE

These delicious cakes are baked in individual muffin cases so they are perfectly portioned. Relatively low in fat, the flavour is all in the banana with texture in the pecans, sultanas and cranberries. They are nutritious and wholesome. I like to have a batch of these available for mid-morning second breakfasts – surely it's never too early to eat cake? They are also great for picnics or packed lunches.

☀ MELTED METHOD

Makes 12

INGREDIENTS

500g (1lb 2oz) ripe bananas (about 4 large bananas)

75g (2¾oz) melted butter

1 teaspoon vanilla bean paste

1 teaspoon grated orange zest

1 egg, beaten

375g (13oz) plain flour

125g (4½oz) golden caster sugar

1 teaspoon baking powder

1 teaspoon bicarbonate of soda

9 medjool dates, stoned and chopped

125g (4½oz) chopped pecans

60g (2oz) golden sultanas or dried cranberries (optional)

Preheat the oven to 180°C (350°F/Gas 4). Place 12 tulip cases in a muffin cake tin.

Mash the bananas in a large bowl with the melted butter, vanilla bean paste, orange zest and beaten egg. In a separate bowl stir together the flour, sugar and raising agents.

Add the chopped dates, pecans and optional dried fruits to the flour and sugar and toss to coat. Tip the flour mixture into the banana mixture and stir until just combined. Divide the mixture evenly between the muffin cases.

Bake for 20 minutes or until golden. Leave to cool for 5 minutes before transferring to a wire rack.

Storage: Store in an airtight container for up to 7 days.

Note: Do not store bananas in the fridge as they will suffer from 'cold shock', turning black and smelly before they have had time to naturally ripen.

"This recipe is a great and quick way to use up overripe or black bananas."

PARSNIP CAKE

This cake is wonderfully moist, sweet and succulent. Here I've used parsnips with their natural sweetness, with apples, walnuts and maple syrup. The name can be a little unappealing, but I would encourage you to try this cake – it is nutritious and wonderfully satisfying. The maple syrup mascarpone frosting is optional – this cake would work well as a traybake cut into squares for lunch boxes and picnics, too.

☀ MELTED METHOD

Makes a 20cm (8 inch) round cake.

INGREDIENTS

175g (6oz) unsalted butter

250g (9oz) demerara sugar

100ml (3½fl oz) maple syrup

3 large eggs

250g (9oz) self-raising flour

2 teaspoons baking powder

2 teaspoons mixed spice

150g (5½oz) parsnips, peeled and grated

1 medium apple, peeled and grated

Grated zest of 1 small orange, plus 2 tablespoons juice

50g (1¾oz) walnuts, roughly chopped

FOR THE MASCARPONE AND MAPLE SYRUP FROSTING

250g (9oz) mascarpone

3 tablespoons maple syrup, plus extra to drizzle

Preheat the oven to 180°C (350°F/Gas 4). Grease and line two 20cm (8 inch) sandwich tins with non-stick baking parchment.

Melt the butter, sugar and maple syrup together in a saucepan over a gentle heat until dissolved and smooth. Remove from the heat and leave to cool slightly. Whisk the eggs into the mixture.

In a separate bowl, sift together the flour, baking powder and mixed spice. Stir this into the cake batter until smooth.

Add the grated parsnip, apple, orange zest and juice and the walnuts and stir until well combined.

Divide the cake mixture between the prepared tins and bake for 25–30 minutes or until the cake is golden brown and the tops spring back when pressed lightly.

Transfer the tins to a wire rack to cool for 5 minutes in the tins before turning out and leaving to cool completely.

To make the frosting: just before serving, stir the maple syrup into the mascarpone.

Place one cake on a serving plate. Spread half the mascarpone frosting over the base cake and place the other cake on top. Spread the remaining frosting on top of the cake and drizzle with maple syrup as the cake is served.

Storage: Keeps for 3 days in an airtight container – preferably in the fridge.

Variation: Substitute half the parsnip with grated carrot.

Be sure to buy authentic maple syrup, not the cheaper maple-flavoured syrup substitute for the best flavour.

Cake conversion tables

HEAVENLY VANILLA CAKE   (see page 44)

INGREDIENTS	15cm (6in) round*	15cm (6in) square or two 10cm (4in) round	20cm (8in) round	20cm (8in) square	25cm (10in) round	25cm (10 in) square or 30cm (12in) round
Self-raising flour	210g (7½oz)	280g (9¾oz)	420g (15oz)	560g (1lb 3½oz)	630g (1lb 6oz)	840g (1lb 9oz)
Golden caster sugar	150g (5½oz)	200g (7oz)	300g (10½oz)	400g (14oz)	450g (1lb)	600g (1lb 5oz)
Unsalted butter	150g (5½oz)	200g (7oz)	300g (10½oz)	400g (14oz)	450g (1lb)	600g (1lb 5oz)
Large free-range eggs	3	4	6	8	9	12
Fresh milk	3 tbsp	4 tbsp	6 tbsp	8 tbsp	9 tbsp	12 tbsp
Vanilla bean paste	1½ tbsp	2 tbsp	3 tbsp	4 tbsp	4½ tbsp	8 tbsp
FOR THE SYRUP						
Water	75ml (3fl oz)	100ml (3½fl oz)	150ml (¼ pt)	200ml (7fl oz)	225ml (8fl oz)	350ml (12fl oz)
Golden caster sugar	60g (2oz)	85g (3oz)	115g (4oz)	170g (6oz)	185g (6½oz)	225g (8oz)
Vanilla bean paste	1 tbsp	1½ tbsp	2 tbsp	2½ tbsp	3 tbsp	3½ tbsp
BAKING TIME	1 hr	1 hr 15 min	1 hr 30 min	1 hr 40 min	1 hr 45 min	1 hr 50 min

* The quantities for a 15cm (6 inch) round cake can also be used to make two 10cm (4 inch) cakes that will need to be baked for 40 minutes.

CHOCOLATE CAKE   (see pages 38–41)

INGREDIENTS	15cm (6in) round*	20cm (8in) round or 15cm (6in) square	25cm (10in) round or 20cm (8in) square	30cm (12in) round or 25cm (10in) square
Plain chocolate (70% cocoa solids) broken into pieces and melted	100g (3½oz)	200g (7oz)	300g (10½oz)	400g (14oz)
Unsalted butter	125g (4½oz)	250g (9oz)	375g (13oz)	500g (1lb 2oz)
Light brown sugar	175g (6oz)	350g (12oz)	525g (1lb 3oz)	700g (1½ lb)
Medium free-range eggs	3	5	7	10
Vanilla bean paste	1 tsp	1½ tsp	2½ tsp	3 tsp
Plain flour (all purpose)	70g (2½oz)	140g (5oz)	210g (7¼oz)	280g (9¾oz)
BAKING TIME	45 min	1 hr	1 hr 20 min	1 hr 40 min

* The quantities for a 15cm (6 inch) round cake can also be used to make two 10cm (4 inch) cakes that will need to be baked for 30 minutes.

LUXURY FRUIT CAKE (see page 74)

INGREDIENTS	15cm (6in) round*	15cm (6in) square	20cm (8in) round	20cm (8in) square	25cm (10in) round	25cm (10in) square	30cm (12in) round	30cm (12in) square	35cm (14in) round
Naturally coloured glacé cherries, halved	105g (3½oz)	135g (4¾oz)	195g (7oz)	250g (9oz)	290g (10oz)	375g (13oz)	415g (14½oz)	540g (1lb 3oz)	585g (1lb 4oz)
Sultanas	105g (3½oz)	135g (4¾ oz)	195g (7oz)	250g (9oz)	290g (10oz)	375g (13oz)	415g (14½ oz)	540g (1lb 3oz)	585g (1lb 4oz)
Raisins	150g (5½oz)	195g (7oz)	270g (9¾oz)	350g (12oz)	290g (10oz)	525g (1lb 3oz)	585g (1lb 4oz)	760g (1lb 10½ oz)	815g (1lb 12oz)
Currants	185g (6¼oz)	235g (8¼oz)	330g (11¼oz)	425g (15oz)	495g (1lb 1oz)	637.5g (1lb 6oz)	710g (1lb 9oz)	925g (2lb)	990g (2lb 3oz)
Brandy	95ml (3fl oz)	125ml (4½fl oz)	175ml (6fl oz)	225ml (7¾fl oz)	260ml (8½fl oz)	335ml (11½fl oz)	375ml (13fl oz)	485ml (17fl oz)	525ml (18½fl oz)
Stem ginger	15g (½oz)	25g (1oz)	30g (1¼oz)	40g (1½oz)	45g (1¾oz)	60g (2¼oz)	65g (2½oz)	85g (3oz)	95g (3¼oz)
Prunes (ready to eat) cut into quarters	45g (1¾oz)	55g (2oz)	80g (3oz)	100g (3½oz)	115g (4oz)	150g (5½oz)	195g (5¾oz)	215g (7½oz)	235g (8½oz)
Medjool dates, pitted and cut into quarters	45g (1¾oz)	55g (2oz)	80g (3oz)	100g (3½oz)	115g (4oz)	150g (5½oz)	165g (5¾oz)	215g (7½oz)	235g (8½oz)
Unsulphured apricots cut into quarters	45g (1¾oz)	55g (2oz)	80g (3oz)	100g (3½oz)	115g (4oz)	150g (5½oz)	165g (5¾oz)	215g (7½oz)	235g (8½oz)
Lerida figs (ready-to-eat) cut into quarters	45g (1¾oz)	55g (2oz)	80g (3oz)	100g (3½oz)	115g (4oz)	150g (5½oz)	165g (5¾oz)	215g (7½oz)	235g (8½oz)
Lemon zest	½	½	1	1	1	1½	2	2½	2½
Orange zest	½	½	1	1	1	1½	2	2½	2½
Dark muscovado sugar	115g (4oz)	145g (5½oz)	200g (7oz)	260g (9¼oz)	300g (10½oz)	390g (13½oz)	435g (15½oz)	565g (1lb 4oz)	605g (1lb 5oz)
Plain flour	105g (3½oz)	135g (4¾oz)	185g (6½oz)	240g (8¾oz)	280g (9¾oz)	360g (12½oz)	400g (14oz)	520g (1lb 2¾ oz)	560g (1lb 4oz)
Baking powder	½ tsp	½ tsp	½ tsp	½ tsp	½ tsp	1 tsp	1 tsp	1½ tsp	1½ tsp
Vanilla extract	¼ tsp	½ tsp	½ tsp	½ tsp	½ tsp	1 tsp	1 tsp	1½ tsp	1½ tsp
Ground cinnamon	¼ tsp	½ tsp	½ tsp	½ tsp	½ tsp	1 tsp	1 tsp	1½ tsp	1½ tsp
Ground ginger	¼ tsp	½ tsp	½ tsp	½ tsp	½ tsp	1 tsp	1 tsp	1½ tsp	1½ tsp
Ground nutmeg	¼ tsp	½ tsp	½ tsp	½ tsp	½ tsp	1 tsp	1 tsp	1½ tsp	1½ tsp
Mixed spice	¼ tsp	½ tsp	½ tsp	½ tsp	½ tsp	1 tsp	1 tsp	1½ tsp	1½ tsp
Unsalted butter	105g (3½oz)	135g (4¾oz)	195g (7oz)	250g (9oz)	290g (10oz)	375g (13oz)	415g (14½ oz)	540g (1lb 3oz)	585g (1lb 4oz)
Eggs (medium-large)	2–3 (weight 115g/4oz)	3 (weight 145g/5½oz)	4 (weight 200g/7oz)	5 (weight 260g/9¼oz)	6 (weight 335g/11¼oz)	7–8 (weight 390g/11½oz)	8–9 (weight 435g/15¼oz)	11–12 (weight 565g/1lb 4oz)	12 (weight 605g/1lb 5oz)
Black treacle	½ tbsp	½ tbsp	1 tbsp	1 tbsp	1 tbsp	1½ tbsp	1½ tbsp	2 tbsp	2½ tbsp
Chopped roasted hazelnuts	45g (1¾oz)	50g (2oz)	80g (3oz)	100g (3½oz)	115g (4oz)	150g (15½oz)	165g (5¾oz)	215g (7½oz)	235g (8½oz)
BAKING TIME	2 hrs	2 hrs	2½ hrs	2½ hrs	2½–3 hrs	2½–3 hrs	3–3½ hrs	3–3½ hrs	3½ hrs

* The quantities for a 15cm (6 inch) round cake can also be used to make two 10cm (4 inch) cakes that will need to be baked for 1 hour 20 minutes.

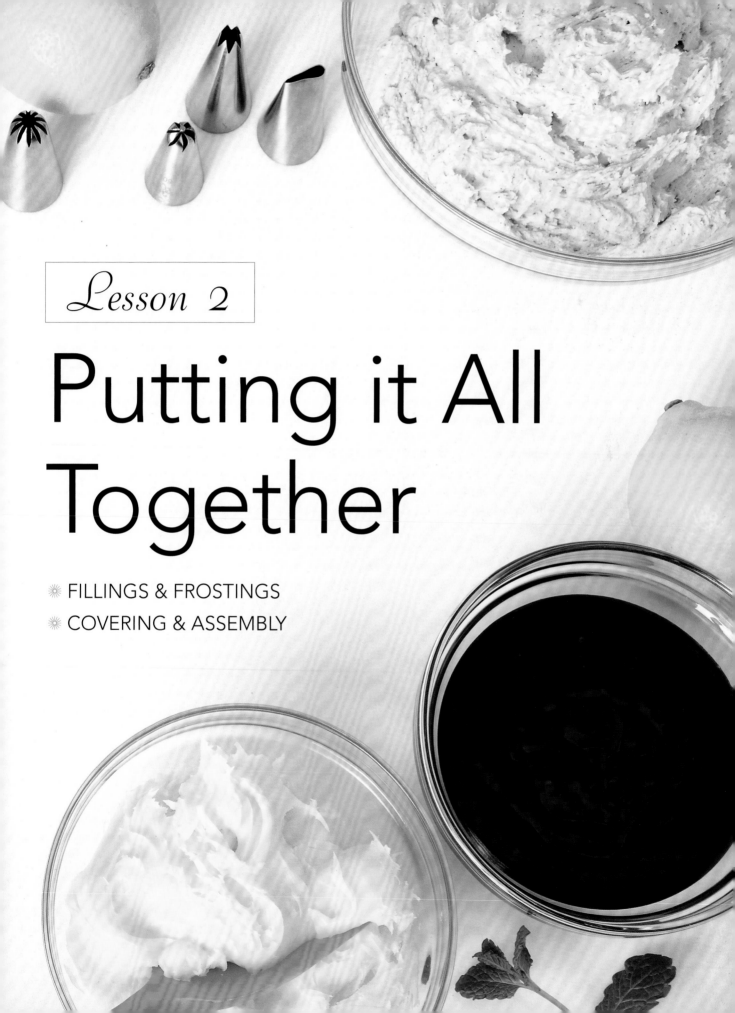

Putting it All Together

* FILLINGS & FROSTINGS
* COVERING & ASSEMBLY

Fillings & Frostings

Once you have mastered the basics of baking the perfect base cake, the next step is to further embellish these cakes with wonderful fillings and frostings. In this chapter I have included fruit purées, citrus curds, buttercreams and ganache. These add extra flavour, colour, texture and presentation to cakes. It is worth experimenting with variations of cakes and fillings to find the combinations that really appeal to you.

1   Preparing a cake for filling

Cakes should be allowed to cool completely before splitting and filling to prevent the butter in the filling and frosting from melting. Use a long serrated knife to cut evenly and cleanly through the cake.

Remove all the baking paper and place the cake on a clean work board. Place one hand on the surface of the cake and position a long serrated palette knife at the desired height held straight. As you begin to cut through the cake with a forwards and backwards sawing action, use the hand on the top of the cake to gently turn the cake in one direction. This will ensure you are always cutting in the same position as the cake turns, which will help in protecting the edges of the cake and ensuring an even cut all the way through the cake. Place a thin acrylic work board between the layers to remove the two halves. Repeat this process if you intend to create several thinner layers from one baked cake.

MICH'S TIP

Use acrylic work boards to handle and manage the cakes as you work.

2 Fruit purée

Fresh berry purées stirred into vanilla buttercream (see page 104) offer an intense burst of summer flavour, as well as adding a wonderful natural colour to simple flavoured cakes such as vanilla, lemon, orange or lime.

Makes 250ml (8½fl oz)

INGREDIENTS

400g (14oz) fresh raspberries

100g (3½oz) golden caster sugar

2 tablespoons water

2–3 teaspoons rose oil or rose water

" *The trick is to ensure the fruit is reduced to concentrate the flavour.* **"**

Place all the ingredients, except the rose oil or water, in a heavy-based saucepan set over a moderate heat. Stir the fruit as it comes to the boil and the sugar dissolves and continue to heat until the fruit has thickened and reduced by one-third. This can take 20–25 minutes.

Transfer the fruit to a heatproof jug and use a hand-held blender to blitz until smooth. Pass the purée through a fine-mesh sieve set over a large bowl. Use the back of a wooden spoon to force the purée through the sieve retaining the seeds. The purée should be thick enough to coat the back of a spatula. Stir in the rose oil or water to taste.

Storage: This will keep in an airtight container in the fridge for up to 2 weeks. It can also be served with ice cream.

3   Citrus curd

Citrus curds – using fresh lemon, lime, orange, passion fruit or a combination – are wonderful by themselves or stirred into buttercreams for a refreshing zesty filling for cakes and roulades. These work really well injected into cupcakes and muffins for extra flavour, texture and colour.

MICH'S TIPS

1 It is important to heat the curd over a pan of simmering water to ensure the eggs are heated and cook so that the curd is stable at ambient temperature.

2 It is important to remove the lemon butter and sugar syrup from the heat before the eggs are added. If the heat is direct, too intense or the lemon syrup too hot, the eggs will scramble.

3 Blending the eggs well before adding them helps to protect the egg white. The egg white albumen protein sets (scrambles) at a much lower temperature than the yolk.

4 Always blend curd with buttercream before filling a cake to be covered with marzipan and icing. This will help stabilize the filling and the cake, else the layers could slip underneath.

Makes 400g (14oz)

INGREDIENTS

90g (3oz) unsalted butter, cubed

225g (8oz) golden caster sugar

Juice of 3 medium lemons, strained

4 medium eggs

Variation: Lime curd – use 150g (5oz) unsalted butter, sugar as above, grated zest and juice of 3 limes, 2 large eggs and 2 egg yolks and follow the method.

Place the butter, sugar and strained lemon juice into a large bowl set over a saucepan of gently simmering water. Heat until the butter has melted and the sugar has dissolved, stirring all the time. Remove the bowl from the heat. In a separate bowl, blend the eggs with an electric hand-held blender until smooth and pour them over the lemon mixture, stirring all the time.

Return the bowl to the heat, placed over the saucepan as before, and continue to heat the curd, stirring with a wooden spoon until thickened – this will take up to 20 minutes. This allows the eggs time to heat slowly, emulsify and stabilize the lemon curd.

Storage: Keep in a bowl, covered with cling film in the fridge for up to 5 days.
Note: Always use Sicilian lemons if you can get hold of them.

LEMON CURD CAKE

Makes a 20cm (8 inch) round cake

INGREDIENTS

300g (10½ oz) unsalted butter, softened

300g (10½oz) golden caster sugar

6 large eggs, beaten

430g (15oz) self-raising flour

6 tablespoons fresh milk

1 tablespoon vanilla bean paste

Grated zest of 4 lemons (juice reserved for the syrup)

FOR THE SYRUP

150ml (¼ pint) freshly squeezed lemon juice passed through a tea strainer

115g (4oz) golden caster sugar

TO DECORATE

6 tablespoons Lemon Curd (see opposite)

1 tablespoon vanilla sugar

Preheat the oven to 160°C (313°F/Gas 2–3). Grease and line a 20cm (8 inch) round cake tin.

The flavour sensation from this lemon cake never fails to impress. A rich butter cake laced with fresh zested lemons, spiked with a lemon syrup and spread with a double layer of homemade lemon curd.

Cream the butter and sugar following the instructions on pages 34–37. Pour the beaten eggs from a jug in a very slow steady stream into the creamed butter and sugar, with the electric whisk on high speed. This will take up to 20 minutes. Remove the electric beater. Sift the flour into the bowl and carefully fold in using a metal spoon or flat-bladed spatula. Stir in the milk, vanilla bean paste and grated lemon zest.

Carefully transfer the mixture to the prepared cake tin and use the back of the spatula to smooth the surface of the cake batter. Bake in the oven for 1½ hours or until the cake is a golden colour and a skewer inserted in the centre comes out clean.

Prepare the syrup as soon as the cake goes into the oven to allow the lemon juice time to dissolve the sugar. Measure the ingredients into a jug and stir occasionally until dissolved.

Spike the cake with a skewer as soon as it comes out of the oven and pour over the syrup. Leave the cake to cool in the tin before turning out and cutting into 3 layers, following the instructions on page 88.

Place the base layer on a serving plate or cake stand and use a flat-bladed palette knife to spread over the lemon curd. Start in the centre and work outwards to the edges. This will keep the filling even and prevent it running down the sides of the cake.

Place the next layer of cake on top and repeat the process until the cake is reassembled with layers of filling. Dust the top of the cake with vanilla sugar.

Storage: Keep in an airtight container at room temperature and eat within 2 days.

MICH'S TIP

This works well as a celebration cake covered with marzipan and sugar paste. Trim the 'dome' off the cake and turn it upside down before splitting. Stir the curd into buttercream before filling.

4 Sauces

Homemade sauces add wonderful flavour to cakes. Stir into buttercreams, cream cheese frostings, cream or drizzle over cakes. They add an indulgent sweetness and help keep cakes moist.

FOR SALTED CARAMEL

Makes about 500g (1lb 2oz)

1 x 397g tin of sweetened condensed milk

175g (6oz) unsalted butter

75g (2¾oz) golden caster sugar

4 tablespoons golden syrup

1–2 teaspoons sea salt, to taste

Used in Coffee Hazelnut Roulade (see page 52)

FOR TOFFEE

Makes 300g (10½oz)

100g (3½oz) golden caster sugar

100g (3½oz) unsalted butter

150ml (¼ pint) double cream

1 teaspoon vanilla extract

2 tablespoons brandy

Used in Sweet Potato Cake (see page 78)

FOR CHOCOLATE

Makes 375g (13oz)

170g (6oz) dark chocolate (70% cocoa solids), broken into pieces

2 tablespoons water

220g (8oz) natural icing sugar

Used in Chocolate Peppermint Brownies (see page 119)

SALTED CARAMEL

Place all the ingredients in a pan. Heat over a medium heat until the butter melts and continue until the caramel comes to the boil. Cook for 8–10 minutes until it has thickened and darkened. Transfer to a clean bowl and leave to cool.
Storage: Keep in the fridge for up to 7 days.

TOFFEE

Preheat a heavy-based pan over a medium heat and add the sugar with the butter dotted on top. Leave to heat, melt and caramelize without stirring. Add the cream and stir until it thickens and caramelizes. Leave to cool. Stir in the vanilla and brandy.
Storage: Keep in the fridge for up to 3 days.

CHOCOLATE

Melt the chocolate and water together in a heavy-based pan. Take off the heat and beat in the icing sugar until smooth. You can also flavour with coffee or peppermint, orange or rose oils.
Storage: Use immediately as this icing sets. Keeps at room temperature for up to 5 days.

Toffee

Salted Caramel

Chocolate

5   Cream-based fillings

Cream-based fillings add mouthfeel, texture and flavour to cakes, gateaux and tortes. They are perfect for cakes made by the whisked method, which are essentially fat-free, as they add moisture and flavour to the cakes. They can easily be flavoured themselves.

FOR THE CREAM CHEESE FROSTING

Makes enough to cover or sandwich and top a 15cm (6 inch) round cake

---

50g (1¾oz) unsalted butter

300g (10½oz) icing sugar

125g (4½oz) cream cheese

Ideal for carrot and other root vegetable cakes.

FOR THE COCONUT CREAM FROSTING

Makes enough to cover or sandwich and top a 15cm (6 inch) round cake

---

300g (10½oz) icing sugar

150g (5½oz) unsalted butter, softened

3 tablespoons creamed coconut, warmed

Ideal for coconut or chocolate cakes.

FOR THE CRÈME CHANTILLY

Makes enough to fill and decorate a 23cm (9 inch) roulade

500ml (17fl oz) whipping cream

125g (4oz) caster sugar

1 tablespoon vanilla bean paste

Ideal for filling roulades, fresh whisked cakes and meringues.

CREAM CHEESE FROSTING

Rub the butter into the icing sugar until it resembles fine breadcrumbs. Beat in the cream cheese until smooth, thick and creamy.
Storage: Make and use immediately, or eat within 2 days. Store in the fridge and eat at room temperature.

COCONUT CREAM FROSTING

Beat together the icing sugar, butter and creamed coconut until smooth.
Storage: Keeps for up to 7 days at room temperature.

CRÈME CHANTILLY

Whip the cream, sugar and vanilla together until voluminous and firm but still glossy. Be careful not to over-whip.
Storage: Keep refrigerated and eat within 2 days.

Cream Cheese Frosting

Crème Chantilly

Coconut Cream Frosting

LIME & PISTACHIO ROULADE WITH CREME CHANTILLY

This whisked sponge is wonderfully light and works well flavoured with the pistachio, zesty lime curd and sweet, silky Crème Chantilly. It is surprisingly easy to make yet impressive served as a pudding or as part of a celebration.

Serves 8–10

INGREDIENTS

30g (1¼oz) butter

4 medium eggs

115g (4oz) golden caster sugar, plus extra to dust

3 tablespoons vanilla bean paste

115g (4oz) plain flour

100g (3½oz) pistachios, roughly chopped

½ quantity Lime Curd (see page 90)

1 quantity Crème Chantilly (see page 93)

TO DECORATE

Grated zest of 1 lime

25g (1oz) pistachios, chopped

Preheat the oven to 180°C (350°F/Gas 4). Line a 23 x 32.5cm (9 x 13 inch) Swiss roll tin with non-stick baking parchment.

MICH'S TIP

The roulade can be made a day in advance and filled prior to serving.

Melt the butter and set aside to cool. Place the eggs and sugar in a large mixing bowl and whisk until the mixture forms a thick trail (about 5 minutes), then briefly whisk in the vanilla bean paste. Sift the flour into the mixture and gently fold in with a metal spoon. Pour in the cooled, melted butter and gently fold until well mixed.

Transfer the batter into the prepared tin, level with the back of a metal spoon and scatter the surface with chopped pistachios.

Bake for 10–12 minutes until risen, golden brown and springy to the touch.

Soak a tea towel with cold water and place on a clean work surface. The tea towel will help to cool the roulade rapidly and create a setting effect – helping the roulade to roll without cracking.

Place a sheet of non-stick baking parchment on top of the tea towel and dust lightly with golden caster sugar. Invert the roulade onto the baking parchment and roll the roulade up tightly, from the short side (as shown on page 53), keeping the baking parchment inside and wrapped in the tea towel. Set aside to cool.

Once cooled, unravel the roulade. Use a palette knife to spread the roulade evenly with Lime Curd followed by a generous layer of Crème Chantilly. Carefully roll the roulade up and transfer to a serving plate. Fill a large piping bag with a closed flower nozzle and the remaining Crème Chantilly (any leftover cream can be served on the side). Pipe a swirled decoration the length of the roulade and decorate with the remaining pistachios and the grated lime zest.

Storage: Best eaten the same day it is filled.

6 Hazelnut praline

Praline is a delicious confection of sweet caramel syrup combined with roasted nuts. Hazelnuts, almonds, cashews and walnuts can all be used. Experiment to find your favourites. Always roast the nuts fresh as you make the praline to enhance the flavour.

Makes about 300g (10½oz)

INGREDIENTS

120g (4½oz) golden caster sugar

240g (8¾oz) roasted, skinned hazelnuts (see page 52)

Place the sugar in a dry, heavy-based saucepan and cook over a moderate heat, stirring with a fork until melted. Continue to cook, without stirring until the sugar is a light caramel. Add the hazelnuts, stirring until well coated. Immediately pour the praline onto a non-stick baking sheet and leave to cool completely. This will take 30 minutes.

Once cooled and set, crush the praline with the base of a rolling pin. Use larger pieces for decoration or blitz in a food processor or chop with a knife to create crushed praline to use within a filling for added crunch.

Storage: Best eaten on the same day.

7   Honeycomb

Also known as cinder toffee, honeycomb is impressive and effective, adding a fizzy, sweet crunch to biscuit cake or as a decoration. It can be fully enrobed in dark chocolate and added as a decoration. However, it cannot be baked once made.

Makes 200–250g (7–9oz)

INGREDIENTS

4 tablespoons golden syrup

200g (7oz) caster sugar

3 teaspoons bicarbonate of soda

Line a baking tray with non-stick baking parchment. Put the golden syrup and sugar in a large saucepan. Bring to the boil, then simmer for 5–10 minutes. The syrup will be ready when a small amount of caramel dropped into a bowl of cold water turns brittle. Do not let the syrup burn. Remove the saucepan from the heat and add the bicarbonate of soda. Quickly mix with a wooden spoon as it will foam up instantly. Pour the honeycomb onto the prepared baking tray and leave it to set and cool (about 30 minutes). Break the honeycomb up into bite-sized chunks with the base of a rolling pin and use for decoration or add to fillings for extra crunch.

Storage: Best eaten on the same day.

DARINA'S RUM & RAISIN CHOCOLATE BISCUIT CAKE

I had the pleasure of welcoming Darina Kelly to the Little Venice Cake Company on an internship. She initiated her arrival with the most delicious chocolate biscuit cake – an indulgently rich no-bake cake held together with melted chocolate, butter and golden syrup. The cake can be packed with many ingredients and can be pressed into any shape and size of cake tin or individual moulds. It is a popular choice as a stable base for celebration and wedding cakes that can be covered with ready-to-roll icing and decorated.

Makes a 15cm (6 inch) round cake or a
1kg (2lb) loaf cake

INGREDIENTS

275g (9¾oz) unsalted butter

150g (5½oz) golden syrup

225g (8oz) dark chocolate (70% cocoa solids)

125g (4½oz) digestive biscuits

125g (4½oz) rich tea biscuits

125g (4½oz) macadamia nuts, roasted and
roughly chopped

125g (4½oz) pistachios, roasted and roughly
chopped

200g (7oz) raisins, soaked in 5 tablespoons
rum for 6 hours

Line a 15cm (6 inch) round cake tin or a 1kg (2lb) loaf tin with cling film brushed with a little groundnut oil (see page 27).

Melt the butter, syrup and chocolate together in a heavy-based saucepan over a moderate heat until smooth. Remove from the heat and leave to cool slightly.

In a separate bowl, roughly crush the biscuits and add the macadamias, pistachios and rum-soaked raisins (or the honeycomb, chocolate drops and marshmallows).

Pour over the chocolate syrup and stir until well mixed. Transfer to the prepared tin and press down well with the back of a metal spoon or rubber spatula. Cover the cake with cling film and place in the fridge overnight to set.

Turn the cake tin upside down and gently shake until the cake is released. Peel away the cling film.

Storage: This cake keeps for up to 5 days at room temperature – or store in the fridge for added crunch!

VARIATION: HONEYCOMB CHOCOLATE BISCUIT CAKE

275g (9¾oz) unsalted butter

150g (5½oz) golden syrup

225g (8oz) chocolate (mixture of 70% cocoa solids dark chocolate and milk chocolate)

125g (4½oz) digestive biscuits

125g (4½oz) rich tea biscuits

250g (9oz) Honeycomb (see page 97), crushed

100g (3½oz) white chocolate drops

125g (4½oz) mixed pink and white marshmallows, cut into quarters

Use these ingredients to follow the method above.

MICH'S TIPS

You could also spread the mixture in a 20 x 30cm (8 x 12 inch) traybake tin and cut into squares once set for picnics and lunch boxes (serves 16).

Roast the nuts and leave to cool before adding to the mixture to enhance the flavour and texture.

Delicious served in bite-size pieces for an after dinner or morning coffee indulgence.

8 Dark chocolate ganache

This fail-safe method for making dark chocolate ganache will ensure you have the backbone for many recipes as it can be used as a filling and frosting, either by itself, whipped or blended with buttercream; as a covering, either poured for a smooth finish or applied with a palette knife for added texture; or hand piped to complete the decoration on many cakes, roulades and gateaux.

Makes 700g (1lb 5oz)

INGREDIENTS

400g (14oz) dark chocolate (70% cocoa solids), broken into pieces

200g (7oz) unsalted butter, cut into pieces

100ml (3½fl oz) double cream

Place the chocolate and butter together in a large bowl and microwave for 60 seconds on high to begin the melting process. Place the cream in a heavy-based saucepan and bring to the boil. As the cream is boiling, remove from the heat and pour over the chocolate and butter.

Start stirring with a rubber spatula and continue to work the cream until the ganache becomes silky, smooth and very glossy.

The ganache can be used in this state for pouring (see page 111) over cakes that have been skim-coated (see page 107). Leave the ganache to cool and thicken slightly to use in buttercream for hand piping or palette knifing over and around a skim-coated cake. Whip cooled ganache with an electric whisk to aerate the ganache and then use by itself for a rich filling in recipes.

VARIATION: CHOCOLATE GANACHE BUTTERCREAM

For an indulgent chocolate buttercream, mix together 1 quantity of Vanilla Buttercream (see page 104) and 250g (9oz) cooled chocolate ganache (or to taste) in a large bowl with a wooden spoon until smooth.

MICH'S TIPS

1 The ganache should be cooled to room temperature before adding to buttercream. This avoids melting the butter in the buttercream.

2 For a less intense chocolate buttercream add less chocolate ganache.

Storage: Keep in an airtight container in the fridge for up to 2 weeks, or in the freezer for 3 months. Defrost at room temperature and warm in a microwave or over a pan of simmering water.

9 White chocolate ganache

White chocolate ganache is wonderfully creamy and sweet. It can be quite temperamental and unstable so I would only recommend using it as a filling for a cake that you are intending to eat straight away and not to be considered for covering with marzipan and icing. Use the best-quality white chocolate available.

Makes 600g (1lb 5oz)

INGREDIENTS

300ml (½ pint) double cream

45g (1½ oz/3 tablespoons) glucose syrup

400g (14oz) white chocolate, broken into pieces or chocolate buttons

75g (2¾oz) unsalted butter

Place the double cream with the glucose syrup in a small saucepan and bring to the boil. Measure the chocolate into a large bowl. Once the cream is boiling, remove from the heat and pour over the chocolate. Leave to stand, without stirring, for 5 minutes, then stir until smooth.

VARIATIONS

These two alternative methods for making white chocolate ganache are more simple, but have limitations.

1 Melt 300g (10½oz) white chocolate, cool, then whip in 300ml (½ pint) double cream until thick and glossy. This can be used to cover a cake but is not stable at room temperature as the cream has not been heated. It must be eaten within 4 hours or stored in the refrigerator.

2 Boil 300ml (½ pint) double cream, then pour it over 300g (10½oz) white chocolate in a bowl. Stir until smooth, then leave to cool.

Note: White chocolate does not contain cocoa solids, it consists of cocoa butter, sugar, milk solids and salt.

As the ganache cools stir in the unsalted butter. Leave the ganache to cool and thicken and use to sandwich between layers of cake.

Storage: This ganache can be kept in the refrigerator for up to 7 days. Remove and allow to come up to room temperature for 30 minutes to soften before using.

10 Vanilla buttercream

Buttercream made with softened unsalted butter and icing sugar is the safest, sweetest filling to include between layers of cake. Buttercream is stable at room temperature and can be combined with a host of other flavours to create exciting, interesting tastes. It is important to use butter that has been left to soften to cream well.

Makes 750g (1lb 10oz)

INGREDIENTS

250g (9oz) unsalted butter, softened

500g (1lb 2oz) unrefined icing sugar (or pure white icing sugar)

2 tablespoons vanilla bean paste

Place the softened butter in the bowl of an electric mixer and beat for 1 minute until smooth. Turn the speed down and gently add the icing sugar (which does not need to be sifted). Increase the speed of the mixer and continue to mix until the buttercream is pale, creamy and doubled in size.

Add the vanilla bean paste and continue to whisk until fully incorporated.

Storage: This will keep for up to 4 weeks in an airtight container in the fridge. Bring up to room temperature and re-beat before use.

✗ What not to do

Don't be tempted to make buttercream with cold butter – it will not whip up and be very granular. Use real butter rather than a spread. Make the buttercream with unsalted butter, and add a little salt if you prefer.

Don't add milk to the buttercream to slacken it – it will reduce the keeping properties – milk will sour at room temperature over time. If the buttercream is stiff, continue to beat for 5 minutes.

MICH'S TIPS

1 When making buttercream it is a good idea to smother the mixer with a clean cloth as you add the icing sugar to contain the fine sugar dust cloud that is invariably created!

2 Buttercream made with the unrefined icing sugar will have a caramelized colour and flavour and combines beautifully with vanilla bean paste, coffee, caramel, chocolate and praline.

3 Pure white buttercream is the perfect blank canvas for combining with fruit purées and colours.

VARIATIONS

Many flavours, purées, curds, chocolates and ganaches can be added to buttercream. Here are my favourites – to be added to 1 quantity of vanilla buttercream.

FRUIT CITRUS CURDS – Stir in 250g (9oz) homemade lemon, lime or passion fruit curd (see page 90).
FRESH ZESTS – Add 2 tablespoons fine lemon, orange or lime zest. Combine flavours for a St Clement's twist or Lemon and Lime.

FRUIT PURÉES – Add fruit purées to taste as they are in season: raspberry and rose, blackcurrant, mixed summer berries, strawberry and champagne.
WHITE CHOCOLATE – Stir in 200g (7oz) melted white chocolate.
COFFEE – Add a cooled shot of espresso (about 50ml (2fl oz) or dissolve 2 teaspoons coffee granules in 2 tablespoons freshly boiled water and leave to cool.
MOCHA – Combine a shot of espresso into chocolate ganache buttercream (see page 101) for a mocha flavour.

11 How to skim-coat a cake

A skim coat or crumb coat is a covering of buttercream, which acts as a base coat to prepare cakes for a flawless top coat ready for decorating. Buttercream is a good base to use as it can be spread over the sides and top of the cake with a palette knife to both smooth and shape the cake to ensure it has clean, sharp angular surfaces and joins and to prepare the cake so no crumbs will crumble into the top coat, spoiling the finish. Misshapen cakes or novelty shaped cakes benefit from being skim-coated in buttercream to create the perfect base for the top coat.

Makes enough to cover a 20cm (8 inch) round cake

INGREDIENTS

1 x 20cm (8 inch) round cake

½ quantity (or about 350–400g/12–14oz) Chocolate Ganache Buttercream (see Variation, page 101) – this depends on the depth of the cake and whether it is to be split and filled

YOU WILL ALSO NEED

20cm (8 inch) cake board

Trim the cake and turn it upside down onto a cake board the same size as the cake. Starting on the sides, use a flat-bladed palette knife to paddle the buttercream around the sides of the cake, filling all the holes and gaps to create straight sides. Draw the palette knife inwards around the cake to remove the excess buttercream over the top of the sides so that there is a flat top to work with.

Paddle more buttercream over the top of the cake and smooth and level with the palette knife. Transfer the cake to fridge or freezer for 10 minutes until the butter has firmed to the touch. It is now ready for its top coat.

MICH'S TIP

Top coats can include more hand-piped buttercream decorations, poured ganache, ready-to-roll icing or chocolate sugar paste. This method would be the same if you were using a Swiss meringue buttercream (see page 124).

CHOCOLATE & LIME CAKE

Chocolate and limes have a wonderful affinity. I have stacked 3 tiers of chocolate cake here, layered with lime curd and chocolate ganache buttercream. This cake would make a super centrepiece at a summer garden party – kept out of direct sunlight of course! Substitute the lime curd with raspberry and rose purée and dress the cake with fresh berries for a simple summer wedding or anniversary cake, or try baking the cake with orange zest and add orange oil in the ganache, lustred with gold for a spectacular Christmas centrepiece celebration.

Serves 16–20 as a pudding or 30–40 as finger portions

INGREDIENTS

1 x 10cm (4 inch) single layer Chocolate Cake (see pages 38–41), baked and cooled

1 x 15cm (6 inch) single layer Chocolate Cake (see page 38–41), baked and cooled

1 x 20cm (8 inch) single layer Chocolate Cake (see page 38–41), baked and cooled

1 quantity Lime Curd (see page 90), chilled

1 quantity Chocolate Ganache Buttercream (see Variation, page 101), at room temperature

2 quantities Dark Chocolate Ganache (see page 100), cooled and left to thicken with 2 tablespoons lime oil added, to taste

Fresh limes and gardenia leaves, to decorate

YOU WILL ALSO NEED

1 x 10cm (4 inch), 1 x 15cm (6 inch) and 1 x 20cm (8 inch) round cake boards

1 x 27.5cm (11 inch) cake board edged with 15mm (⅛ inch) brown grosgrain ribbon

Disposable piping bag fitted with a star nozzle

Trim the cakes and turn them upside down onto a cake board the same size as each cake. Split and sandwich each cake with Lime Curd and Chocolate Ganache Buttercream. Skim-coat each layer with buttercream (see page 107). Transfer the cakes to the fridge or freezer for 10 minutes until the butter has firmed to the touch. Spread a little lime-flavoured chocolate ganache onto the centre of the base board. This will hold the cake in position and stop it moving around as it sets.

Place the layered cake in the centre of the base board. Use a flat-bladed palette knife to paddle the lime-flavoured ganache over the top and sides of the cake until it is completely covered. Create interesting shapes with the chocolate ganache using your knife along the way. Stack (see pages 154–155) the next tier directly on top and repeat, finishing with the top tier. Fit a disposable piping bag with a star nozzle and fill it with ganache. Pipe a decorative border around the base tier, then decorate with fresh limes and gardenia leaves.

MICH'S TIPS

1 It is important to work quite quickly when covering the cake with chocolate ganache as the cold temperature of the chilled cake will encourage the ganache to set.

2 It is not necessary to dowel these tiers as they are relatively small, lightweight and the difference between the tiers minimal, so overall the weight is evenly distributed.

12 Pouring ganache

My ganache recipe handles beautifully for pouring evenly over skim-coated cakes thanks to the butter content. Once covered the ganache is stable at ambient or room temperature and does not need to be refrigerated. It will keep for 5 days. The cake should be chilled and the ganache warm to have the best effect.

Makes enough to cover a 20cm (8 inch) cake

INGREDIENTS

1 x 20cm (8 inch) round baked and cooled Chocolate Cake (see pages 38–41), skim-coated with Chocolate Ganache Buttercream (see page 101)

I quantity Dark Chocolate Ganache (see pages 100–101)

Skim-coat the cake using the buttercream following the instructions on page 107. Remove the cake from the freezer and place on a wire rack set over a sheet of non-stick baking parchment. Use a ladle to spoon generous spoonfuls of ganache over the top of the cake.

Use the base of the ladle to swirl the ganache outwards to the edge of the cake and down over the sides. The ganache can be ladled from side to side to ensure even coverage. Be careful not to press too hard with the ladle to avoid disturbing the buttercream underneath.

Once all the top and sides are covered pick the wire rack up with two hands and repeatedly and firmly tap back down onto the table to smooth and even the ganache. Leave to set for a few minutes.

Carefully lift the cake from the wire rack and use a small sharp knife to remove the curtains of chocolate ganache hanging beneath the base of the cake. Place carefully onto a cake board or cake stand to completely set. Allow the remaining ganache to cool and use it to pipe extra decoration on your cake.

> *"It is imperative cakes are placed on boards the same size as the cakes to be able to handle them."*

13   Macro piping

Macro piping with cream-based frostings, larger nozzles and disposable piping bags are a great introduction to hand piping to build confidence. Macro piping requires less precision than the more intricate royal icing (see pages 166–168) – perfect for decorating cupcakes, gateaux, tortes and roulades. Cupcakes require relatively little time, expertise and expensive equipment to achieve a fabulous result.

HOW TO PREPARE FOR MACRO PIPING

Snip the base off the disposable piping bag and insert a nozzle. Roll the back of the bag down to create a stiff cone. Hold the inner cone and spoon the frosting inside until half full. Roll the outside of the bag up and massage the frosting down to the nozzle to remove any air pockets. Twist the bag at the top of the frosting to seal and hold the bag vertically with this fist grip to pipe the frosting.

Pipe individual petals, starting with the base and work upwards, holding the thin tip of the nozzle uppermost.

A rosette nozzle creates an elegant swirl, starting from the inside and working outwards.

Pipe an open flower starting in the centre and turn the cake to create the central closed petal. The thinner part of the nozzle should be uppermost.

Pipe small stars to fill the surface, starting from the outside and working inwards.

An open star can be used for a more contemporary swirl. Start from the outside and work inwards.

Progress to this more elaborate rose design using the teardrop nozzle. Pipe individual two-tone petals starting with the base layer and working your way up.

YOU WILL NEED

Cupcakes

Buttercream (see page 104)

Disposable piping bags

A selection of nozzles:
   top row, from left to right:
   No.124, No.822 and No.124
   bottom row, from left to right:
   No.822, No.2C and No.124

Decorating cupcakes can be a great introduction to piping for the beginner. Making, baking and decorating a batch of cupcakes can be very satisfying. They are relatively quick to produce, without having to invest a huge amount in time, energy, equipment and skill. Bake a batch of vanilla cupcakes and experiment with the flavour and decoration on the top. Here I have chosen to make vanilla cupcakes and have decorated them with a white buttercream blended with fresh raspberry and rose purée.

"*I always use disposable piping bags for piping with buttercream as they are more hygienic.*"

TWO-TONE MACRO PIPING

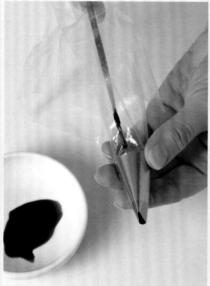

To create a two-tone effect, place your chosen nozzle in a large disposable piping bag against the seam. Load the end of a paintbrush with edible food colour and draw it up the seam of the bag. Fill the piping bag with buttercream – the colour will concentrate through the buttercream at the seam. Arrange your decorated cupcakes in liners and present them on a pretty cake stand or in gift boxes.

PIPED GANACHE LEAVES AND SHELLS

For the leaves: snip the end of the piping bag and fit a No.69 nozzle, then fill with ganache. Hold the bag in two hands, the nozzle held with the split horizontally, and apply pressure without moving the bag. This will build up the back of the leaf. Slowly bring the nozzle towards you, maintaining the pressure. Once you have the size and shape of the leaf you like, release the pressure completely and gently lift the nozzle up and away from the leaf to form the tip.

For the shells: snip the end of the piping bag, fit an open star nozzle and fill with ganache. Hold the nozzle at a 45 degree angle and pipe a shell. Release the pressure as you draw the bag around the cake, then start the next shell by applying pressure over the tail of the previous shell. Repeat all around the base.

Always allow ganache to cool and stiffen to piping consistency. This shell decoration is perfect for sealing the base of any cake or gateau. If the ganache becomes too stiff to pipe, simply warm in a microwave to soften.

RASPBERRY ROSE CAKE

Decorating this cake with different intensities of raspberry and rose buttercream can be achieved in under an hour, yet looks impressive enough to take centre stage at any celebration. I love the height of the cake and the fact the colour is provided purely from the fresh raspberries rather than adding artificial colours. There are so many variations once you have mastered this.

Makes a 2-tiered 15cm (6 inch) round cake

INGREDIENTS

2 x 15cm (6 inch) round Heavenly Vanilla Cakes (see pages 44 and 82)

Vanilla Buttercream (see page 104) made with 750g (1lb 10oz) butter and 1.5kg (3lb 6oz) white icing sugar

1 quantity Raspberry and Rose Purée (see page 89)

YOU WILL ALSO NEED

1 x 15cm (6 inch) cake board

Large disposable piping bags

4 x 2D nozzles

Bake the cakes as instructed and leave them to cool. Make the buttercream and divide into two bowls. Add 3 tablespoons of purée to one bowl of buttercream.

Trim the top off the vanilla cakes so they are level and sandwich the cakes with the flavoured buttercream, making sure you sandwich the cakes cut side facing inwards.

Place the cake on a cake board and spread the flavoured buttercream over the sides and top to create a smooth, sharp finish. Transfer the cake to the fridge to firm. Keep any remaining flavoured buttercream.

Once chilled, place the cake in the centre of a pretty cake plate or stand. Mark the side of the cake into three even sections with the back of a palette knife.

Divide the unflavoured buttercream evenly between 4 bowls and add purée to 3 of the bowls to create an ever-increasing shade of colour and intensity. Add any flavoured buttercream from the skim coat to the deepest colour.

Fit a large disposable piping bag with a 2D nozzle and fill with the darkest colour buttercream. Start by holding the piping bag with the nozzle a little away from the cake and angle at 90 degrees. Pipe a rose swirl from the centre of the flower outward at the base of the cake. Butt the next swirl against the first and repeat until you have a ring of roses evenly around the base of the cake.

Add any excess of this darkest colour buttercream to the next paler shade bowl and stir evenly. Fill a clean piping bag fitted with the 2D nozzle with this slightly paler colour and repeat the process of piping a ring of roses around the middle of the cake.

Add any excess buttercream to the next paler shade and repeat the piping process for the top ring of piped roses. Finally, mix any excess buttercream with the unflavoured portion so it is barely coloured and fill the top of the cake with hand-piped roses, starting from the outside and working inwards.

Fix a little buttercream
in the centre of the cake
plate or stand before you
place the cake in position
to keep it stable and prevent
it moving around as
you pipe on the roses.

14 Glacé icing

Glacé icing is a simple water icing made by blending icing sugar with water. Citrus juices can be used, or coffee, chocolate and caramel for richer flavour and colour. White and unrefined icing sugars can be used to make glacé icing. It can be used as a simple frosting for cakes, bars and fairy cakes, but is not stable enough to cover a cake intended for additional hand-piped decoration.

Makes about 275g (9¾oz)

INGREDIENTS

250g (9oz) icing sugar

2–3 tablespoons water (or other liquid)

Measure the icing sugar into a large clean bowl. Measure the liquid into a spoon held over the bowl for accuracy. Pour in a little liquid then begin stirring round in circles from the centre out. This will help to incorporate the sugar gradually and prevent lumps forming in the icing. Add more liquid as necessary until the icing reaches the desired consistency. It should be thick enough to coat the back of a spoon, yet thin enough to be drizzled into position.

Storage: Use immediately and discard any leftover glacé icing. Cakes covered with glacé icing can be stored safely at room temperature.

Note: The icing will set to the touch but not be as firm as royal icing. It is possible to pipe simple lines and messages with glacé icing, but more elaborate decoration should be created with royal icing.

Humidity and desired consistency will affect the exact amount of liquid needed. I would advise adding 2 teaspoons of liquid at a time, adjusting with more liquid or sugar if needed.

VARIATIONS

1 Chocolate Glacé Icing – Put 170g (6oz) dark chocolate, broken into pieces and 6 tablespoons water in a small heavy-based saucepan. Heat gently until melted. Beat in 220g (8oz) icing sugar until the icing is smooth.

2 Coffee Glacé Icing – measure 200g (7oz) unrefined icing sugar into a bowl and make a well in the centre. Add 40ml (1½ fl oz) espresso and stir until smooth and thick enough to coat the back of a spoon.

CHOCOLATE PEPPERMINT BROWNIES

We had no idea when we made these just how moreish they would be. Serve these as bite-sized petits fours after a dinner party or serve with fresh mint tea for a sophisticated afternoon tea. Given their success, the variations are endless!

Makes 18 slices or 36 petits fours squares

INGREDIENTS

1 x 20cm (8 inch) Chocolate Cake (see pages 38–41 and 82), but add 100g (3½oz) dark chocolate chips after the flour has been added

1 quantity Chocolate Glacé Icing (see opposite), plus 1 tablespoon peppermint oil stirred in

Pearl lustre (optional)

YOU WILL ALSO NEED

30 x 20cm (12 x 8 inch) baking tin, lined with non-stick baking parchment

Make the brownies following the recipe for a 20cm (8 inch) Chocolate Cake, bake for 35–40 minutes, then leave to cool in the tin. Make the icing and spread it over the brownie as soon as it is ready and still in the tin. Leave to cool and set before removing the brownies from the tin using the paper for support. Cut into slices.

Storage: Store in an airtight container at room temperature for up to 3 days.

FLAVOUR VARIATIONS

1 ORANGE – Add the zest of 2 oranges to the brownie batter before baking and add 1 tablespoon natural orange oil to the chocolate icing.

2 RASPBERRY AND ROSE – Scatter 200g (7oz) fresh raspberries over the base of the tin before pouring in the brownie batter and add 2 teaspoons rose oil to the chocolate icing.

3 WHITE CHOC AND HAZELNUT WITH MOCHA FROSTING – Replace 100g (3½oz) choc chips with 100g (3½oz) chopped white chocolate; add 75g (2¾oz) roasted, chopped hazelnuts. For the icing: replace half the water with espresso.

15 Italian meringue

Italian meringue is a stable meringue at room temperature made by pouring a slow steady stream of hot sugar syrup into freshly whisked egg whites to cook and stabilize the meringue. I use a blow torch to caramelize the sugar in the meringue to add colour as a finishing touch. This meringue requires no further cooking and can be used to add a silky frosting to cakes, tarts and roulades.

Makes enough to cover and decorate a 20cm (8 inch) cake (about 450g/1lb)

INGREDIENTS

300g (10oz) white caster sugar

25g (1oz) liquid glucose

65ml (2½fl oz) water

4 medium egg whites

YOU WILL ALSO NEED

A sugar thermometer

Measure the sugar, glucose and water into a saucepan and heat over medium high heat, stirring gently. Use a pastry brush dipped in cold water to remove sugar crystals that may build up around the edge of the saucepan. Place the sugar thermometer in the sugar solution and stop stirring as the temperature reaches 80°C (176°F). Continue heating without stirring until the temperature reaches 110°C (230°F).

Put the egg whites in a clean bowl attached to an electric whisk and start whisking on full speed. As the syrup reaches 119°C (246°F) remove the pan from the heat and, with the egg whites still on full speed, add the syrup to the egg whites in a slow, steady stream – be careful not to catch the blade of the whisk with the syrup as it is poured in. Once all the syrup has been added, whisk until the meringue has cooled.

Storage: Use immediately to cover and decorate a cake.

"I use Italian meringue to decorate the outside of cakes, cupcakes, pies and tarts that require no further baking as it holds its shape well."

MICH'S TIP

It is imperative the temperatures and methods are accurately adhered to when making Italian meringue as the boiling sugar syrup carefully cooks the egg whites so the meringue is stable at ambient temperature. Not reaching the right temperatures, or adhering to the method will result in an unstable meringue that may not be safe to eat.

STRAWBERRY CHIFFON CAKE

Chiffon cake is wonderfully light – combining an oil-based batter with an egg white foam. It can be refrigerated as the oil helps to keep the cake soft. It has a bland flavour so works well with strong flavoured accompaniments such as fresh strawberries. The cake is smothered in a luxurious Italian meringue, adding a sweet, velvet richness to the cake, and protecting the cake to prevent it drying out. This cake is impressive and fun to make – requiring a sugar thermometer and a blow torch!

Serves 12–16

FOR THE CHIFFON

270g (9½oz) plain flour

300g (10½oz) granulated sugar

2¼ teaspoons baking powder

¾ teaspoon salt

120ml (4fl oz) sunflower oil

7 large egg yolks plus 9 large egg whites

180ml (6fl oz) whole milk

½ teaspoon cream of tartar

2 teaspoons vanilla bean paste

TO DECORATE

1 quantity Italian Meringue (see page 120)

400g (14oz) fresh strawberries

100g (3½oz) toasted flaked almonds

YOU WILL ALSO NEED

a 25cm (10 inch) tube pan (unlined)

a No.195 open rosette nozzle

Preheat the oven to 170°C (325°F/Gas 3).

Mix together the flour, 150g (5½oz) of the sugar, baking powder and salt. In a separate bowl whisk together the oil, egg yolks and milk. Add the flour mixture to the egg yolk mixture and whisk until combined.

Beat the egg whites on high speed until frothy. Add the cream of tartar and vanilla paste and continue whisking until soft peak stage. Gradually add the remaining sugar and beat until stiff and glossy (about 5 minutes).

Whisk one-third of the meringue (foam) into the flour batter. Gently fold in the remaining foam until combined. Pour the batter into the tin and bake for 50–60 minutes until risen, golden and a knife inserted comes away clean.

Remove the cake from the oven and suspend the tin over an upturned bowl until cool.

Run a knife around the inside of the tin to loosen the cake and carefully remove the cake from the tin. Trim the base and place on a cake stand. Prepare the Italian Meringue following the instructions on page 120 and use a palette knife to paddle meringue over the top and sides of the cake until the surface is completely coated.

Spoon the remaining Italian meringue into a piping bag fitted with large open rosette nozzle (No. 195). Pipe rosettes around the top of the cake in a circular motion. Make sure you hold the piping bag vertically over the cake. Press toasted flaked almonds around the base of the cake. Use a blow torch to gently caramelize the Italian meringue – take care not to burn the peaks of the meringue. Fill the centre of the cake with fresh strawberries.

Storage: This cake will keep for 2 days in the fridge.

For added decadence, split and fill the chiffon cake with homemade lemon curd (see page 90) or strawberry jam before covering with meringue.

16 Swiss meringue buttercream

This Swiss meringue buttercream relies on heating the sugar and egg whites together to make a meringue into which butter is beaten to thicken and stabilize it. This buttercream has a wonderfully silky, velvety texture that is also deliciously light. It handles beautifully for piping onto cupcakes and larger cakes and holds its shape well. Because the meringue is heat treated, this buttercream is stable at room temperature.

Makes 1kg (2¼lb) enough to cover 48 mini cupcakes, 24 larger cupcakes or to cover and decorate a 25cm (10 inch) cake

INGREDIENTS

5 medium egg whites at room temperature

275g (9¾oz) golden caster sugar

450g (1lb) unsalted butter

2 teaspoons vanilla bean paste

Storage: This buttercream keeps well at room temperature, decorated over a cake for 2–3 days.

Put the egg whites and sugar into a large clean bowl over a pan of gently simmering water. Whisk with an electric hand-held whisk until the meringue is silky and not grainy when a little is rubbed between your finger and thumb – you are looking for a temperature of 88°C (190°F). This should take about 10 minutes.

MICH'S TIPS

1 Because the meringue is cooked it is stable at room temperature.

2 Leave the meringue to cool to room temperature before adding the butter otherwise it could split. If this happens continue to whisk, then leave to cool.

3 The meringue may loosen as you add the first butter, keep adding more – it will thicken!

Use a good-quality
dark chocolate (with at
least 70% cocoa solids)
to create a decadent,
rich chocolate flavour.

Remove the meringue from the heat but continue to whisk until the meringue cools to room temperature and has thickened. Add the butter in small batches and beat well between each addition. Add the vanilla and whisk until well combined.

TO MAKE CHOCOLATE MERINGUE BUTTERCREAM

Add 190g (6½oz) melted, cooled dark chocolate (70% cocoa solids) to the swiss meringue buttercream. Whisk in with an electric hand-held whisk until the buttercream is silky and smooth.

CHOCOLATE MINI ADVENT BITES

Makes 48 mini cupcakes

INGREDIENTS

125g (4½oz) unsalted butter

175g (6oz) light brown sugar

3 medium eggs

100g (3½oz) dark chocolate (70% cocoa solids), melted and cooled

2 teaspoons vanilla extract

70g (2½oz) plain flour

50g (1¾oz) dried cherries, soaked in 2 tablespoons rum for 1 hour

50g (1¾oz) glacé cherries, washed and chopped

Grated zest of 1 orange

1 quantity Chocolate Meringue Buttercream (see page 125)

Edible gold shimmer dust

YOU WILL ALSO NEED

2 x 24-hole mini-muffin tins

mini cupcake liners

Disposable piping bag fitted with a 2D nozzle

Preheat the oven to 160°C (313°F/Gas 2–3). Fill the holes of the mini muffin tins with mini cupcakes liners.

We first served these mini advent bites at my annual Christmas masterclass held at London's Dorchester hotel. They certainly set the scene for the run up to Christmas. Decadent but delicate.

Use the butter, sugar, eggs, chocolate, vanilla extract and flour to make the cake mixture following the method on pages 38–41.

Stir the cherries, any remaining rum and the orange zest into the cake batter. Spoon the mixture into a large disposable piping bag and snip the end.

Pipe the batter into the cupcake liners until they are three-quarters filled, then bake in the preheated oven for 10 minutes.

Transfer the muffin tins to a wire rack, leave to cool, then remove the cakes from the tin to the wire rack to cool completely.

Half-fill a large disposable piping bag fitted with a 2D nozzle with the Chocolate Meringue Buttercream. Pipe a generous swirl of buttercream on top of each cupcake.

Keep the nozzle held vertically over the cupcakes. Start in the centre then pull the bag out and around to fill the surface. Finish by releasing the pressure and tail off with a flick. Dust the cupcakes with gold dust.

Storage: Keep in an airtight container at room temperature for up to 3 days.

VARIATION

Stir 2 tablespoons of rum and 2 teaspoons of ground cinnamon through the Swiss Meringue Buttercream (see page 124) and finish with a dusting of ground cinnamon.

CHOCOLATE BASKET WEAVE CAKE

The technique for this icing is far simpler than it may look – it is very easy to achieve a great result with a little practice. For a variation, use Swiss meringue buttercream over a vanilla, lemon or orange cake and decorate with fresh summer berries.

Makes a 20cm (8 inch) decorated cake

INGREDIENTS

1 x 20cm (8 inch) round Chocolate Cake (see pages 38–41 and 82)

2 quantities Chocolate Meringue Buttercream (see page 125)

40–50 chocolate truffles (about 520g/1lb 3oz)

YOU WILL ALSO NEED

Disposable piping bags

a No.4 and a No.47 weave nozzle

Skim-coat the baked chocolate cake with half the buttercream following the technique on page 107.

Fill 2 disposable piping bags, one fitted with a plain No. 4 nozzle and the other a No. 47 weave nozzle, with the remining buttercream.

Begin by piping a vertical line using the No. 4 nozzle from the top edge of the cake to the base. Hold the basket weave nozzle with the combed teeth facing outwards, smooth side nearest the cake. Pipe 2cm (¾ inch) horizontal lines across the vertical line from left to right with a wave/fold at the start, tailing off at the end. These lines should be at intervals down the side of the cake the same width as each piped basket weave stripe. Pipe a second vertical line top to bottom, piping over the tails of the first weave stripes.

Take the basket weave nozzle and pipe a second row of basket weave stripes in between the first, making sure the start of each butts up to, but does not cross over, the vertical line previously hand piped. Repeat all around the cake until the sides are completely covered and decorated. Dress the cake with your favourite truffles.

Storage: Keep in a cake tin at room temperature and eat within 3 days.

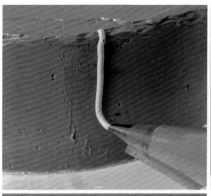
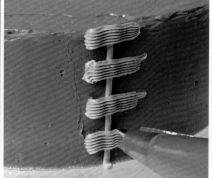
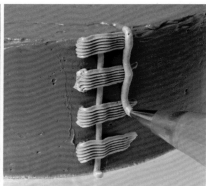
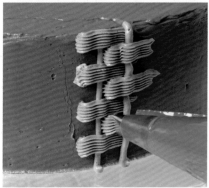

MICH'S TIPS

1 Maintain the pressure as you work around the cake so each vertical line and basket weave stripe is even. Be sure to keep straight rows and columns as you work around the cake so the design finishes evenly.

2 Start at the back of the cake so any discrepancy in the join will be hidden at the back.

17 Royal icing

Royal icing is made from icing sugar and egg white. The strength of the albumen (egg white protein) means the icing can be whisked up into a wonderfully mallow, glossy icing with a good viscosity and elasticity that allows it to be used to cover and decorate cakes. The icing will set firm, hard and somewhat brittle as the icing dries. It has been the traditional covering for wedding cakes since the mid 19th century, when royalty and nobility began covering cakes with royal icing as a status of wealth and purity. Today, it is more common to cover cakes with ready-to-roll icing, also known as sugar paste or fondant (not to be confused with the pouring fondant) and then decorated with hand-piped royal icing decoration.

Makes 1.5kg (3lb 6oz)

INGREDIENTS

7 egg whites (fresh or lightly pasteurized)

About 1kg (2½lb) icing sugar

Freshly squeezed juice of 2 lemons

Leave the egg whites to come up to room temperature for 1 hour in the bowl of an electric mixer, covered with a clean cloth, before making the royal icing. Once at room temperature, begin whisking on slow speed. Increase the speed until the egg whites reach the soft peak stage.

When soft peaks are clearly seen, stop the mixer and add the icing sugar. Whisk on super slow speed until the icing sugar is incorporated, then on high speed until the icing is mallow, glossy, aerated and has the consistency of freshly whipped double cream.

"Add the lemon juice passed through a tea strainer to remove any pips or lemon flesh."

Pass the lemon juice through a tea strainer and add to the bowl. Continue to whisk for 2 minutes. The icing should be glossy, thick and wonderfully mallow.

Storage: Royal icing once made will keep in an airtight container for up to 7 days. Re-whisk daily before use.

MICH'S TIPS

1 Royal icing is relatively inexpensive. I would make this in a large enough batch to be practical in an electric mixer. Smaller quantities are just not sensible for this size of machine.

2 Look for cartons of lightly pasteurized egg white available in the chilled section of the supermarket. These are safe, have up to 1 month's shelf life unopened, and a 7-day shelf life once opened if kept refrigerated. The cartons can also be frozen and defrosted for use as required. They are generally less expensive than purchasing fresh eggs, safer and more convenient to use.

3 The lemon juice strengthens the icing, helps to keep it white and imparts a subtle flavour.

4 Once you have made the royal icing, if it looks grainy or really stiff, add a little more egg white and continue to whisk for 2 minutes on high speed.

COLOURING

Once the royal icing has been made to the correct consistency it can be coloured. Transfer the desired amount to a separate bowl. Add colour gel with a cocktail or wooden stick. Start with a small amount. Stir the colour into the icing with the back of a spoon to avoid adding air bubbles to the icing. Add more colour gel to increase the colour concentration or blend colours to make your own shade. The colour should be evenly distributed and smooth. Cover the bowl with a clean damp cloth or transfer the icing to an airtight container.

MICH'S TIP

Royal icing will start to dry and crust over as soon as it is exposed to air. Be sure to cover the bowl of icing with a clean damp cloth or transfer to airtight containers.

"Only pipe with royal icing made with egg white, not thinned down with water."

FOR FLOODING

Add a little cold water, a drop at a time, to coloured royal icing to thin it down for flooding icing to be used in lettering, run outs and shapes (see pages 182–183). Add the water until the icing can be trailed on the top to leave a ribbon that has settled and disappeared by the count of ten.

GLYCERINE FOR COVERING

Royal icing can be used to cover cakes. It is advisable to add 1 tablespoon of glycerine to 1 batch of royal icing. This will ensure the icing sets firm but can still be cut easily with a knife to avoid being too brittle and shattering.

"Don't be tempted to thicken flooding icing with more icing sugar in order to pipe with it. The proportion of egg white albumen will be too low, resulting in soft, crumbly icing."

Covering & Assembly

For a **special** occasion, cakes can be filled and then covered with marzipan, ready-to-roll **sugar paste**, chocolate, **fondant** or royal icing as the perfect blank canvas, before further embellishing with intricate hand piping, **hand painting** or hand moulding. In this chapter, I will show you how to achieve a flawless, **professional** finish with your covering to create the perfect covered cake. **Be patient** – results will improve with practice.

1 Preparing marzipan/almond paste for covering

Marzipan or almond paste is a versatile ingredient in cake covering. It is made from ground almonds and sugar. Look for the highest quality marzipan available – up to 36% ground almonds with no added colouring or flavouring.

YOU WILL NEED

Marzipan

Icing sugar

Rolling pin

Icing smoothers

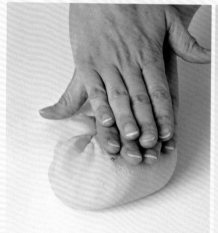

It is important to knead marzipan to make it soft, pliable and ready to roll and cover smoothly. Begin kneading by turning the marzipan in a clockwise direction, bringing the outside edge into the centre and pressing down with the fingertips. Don't be tempted to use the heel of your hand here as it will press down too hard and introduce air. When the marzipan is ready to roll it should feel soft and pliable without being sticky and have formed into a smooth ball.

Flip the marzipan over so the folds are tucked underneath. It is now ready to roll.

✕ What not to do

Do not automatically dust the work surface with icing sugar before you start. This will dry the marzipan out which would encourage cracking, make the marzipan sweeter and in very hot weather or with very hot hands become sticky.

Do not turn the marzipan over or pull it into folds as you knead it. This will introduce plates and folds in the marzipan that will form creases, tears or air bubbles as you come to roll it out.

If the marzipan is sticking as you attempt to roll, dust your hands with a little icing sugar and rub this down the length of the rolling pin.

THE BENEFITS OF USING MARZIPAN

1 The natural oil in the almonds helps to lock the moisture into cakes as it acts as a water-resistant barrier protecting the cake from drying out.

2 Marzipan dries to give the cake a firm shape and structure, making it more stable before covering with the top coat. This is essential in dowelling cakes for stacking and tiering.

3 Marzipan is used to cover cakes to prevent the colour of the cake bleeding through to the icing layer. This is particularly so when covering a rich fruit cake with royal icing.

4 It complements well with other cake flavours to enhance the overall taste.

Liberally dust the work surface with icing sugar at this stage. You should only roll out the marzipan once so you want to make sure it does not stick. Place the marzipan in the centre of the work surface – ensuring you have enough clear space around to be able to roll the marzipan to the desired size. Hold the rolling pin with both hands and beginning rolling with short, sharp strokes.

It is important to turn the marzipan through 90 degrees every few strokes to ensure the marzipan is rolled evenly and the shape maintained. Keep the marzipan in contact with the work surface, using both your hands to shuffle it around and keep it moving freely. Do not turn the marzipan over.

Continue to roll out until you reach the desired size. As the sheet gets larger use your full hands and arms to the elbow to maintain a smooth rolling action so ridges don't form in the marzipan.

"It's important to know how to handle marzipan to get the best out of it."

Marzipan should be stored at room temperature in a sealed bag to prevent it drying out and becoming crumbly.

✕ What not to do

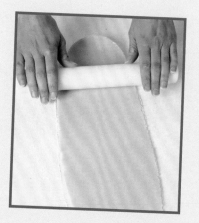

Don't just roll in one direction as you start to roll out the marzipan. This will create a slipper shape of marzipan – long and thin – which can't be used to successfully cover the cake.

Don't press the rolling pin down as you roll. This will introduce ridges in the marzipan. Practise long sweeping strokes with the rolling pin to keep the marzipan smooth.

Don't turn the marzipan over as you roll it – this will introduce too much icing sugar into the marzipan and the creases will form on the surface, drying it out.

Don't take the rolling pin over the edge of the marzipan onto the work surface. This will misshape the marzipan and give a false measurement of the thickness of the marzipan, making it much thinner on the edges.

MICH'S TIP

If you really dislike marzipan or have an allergy, a single tier celebration cake can be covered with two layers of slightly thinner icing. For a wedding cake, substitute one tier with a faux decorated tier and bake a separate, single tier cutting cake that can be covered and served with a single layer of icing.

"Aim for a thickness of 4mm (¼ inch); too thin and the marzipan will tear."

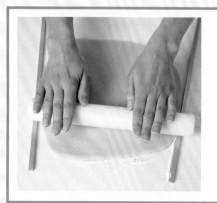

MICH'S TIP

For additional security, place thickness guides either side of the marzipan, which act as tramlines for the rolling pin to roll on to ensure the thickness is even.

Run a smoother over the surface of the marzipan to even it out. This will ensure the marzipan is even and smooth before using to cover the cake.

When the marzipan is the correct size, ensure it is still free flowing (i.e. not sticking to the work surface) and run a smoother over the top of the marzipan with firm purpose. This will even out and smooth any undulations that may still occur in the marzipan.

Use one hand to gently lift the marzipan closest to you, then with the other arm held straight, palm flat and face up, shoot this arm underneath the marzipan to support it.

Place the other arm and palm underneath the marzipan next to the first and open the fingers to increase the surface area and support the marzipan. You are now ready to lift the marzipan off the work surface and onto and over the cake.

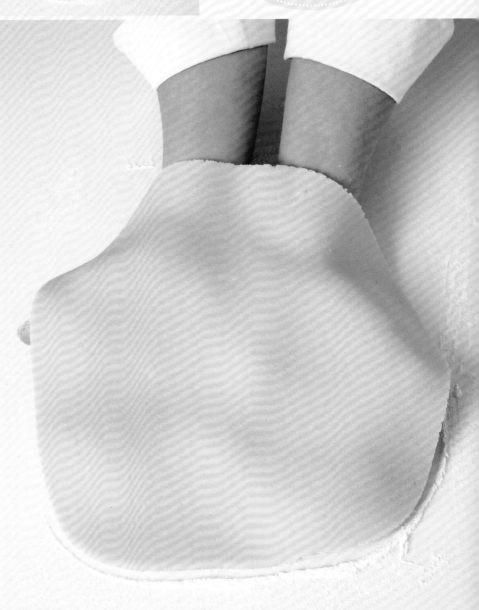

2 Covering with marzipan

Cakes should be baked and cooled before attempting to cover with marzipan. Any heat left in the cake will create moisture underneath the marzipan layer, which will encourage mould and bacteria growth. Cakes should be trimmed to create a level, stable surface and upturned ready to be covered with marzipan

INGREDIENTS

1 x 15cm (6 inch) round cake

500g (1lb 2oz) marzipan, prepared for covering (see pages 136–139)

Apricot jam, sieved and boiled

YOU WILL ALSO NEED

1 x 15cm (6 inch) round cake drum

Round edge icing smoother

Straight edge icing smoother

Note: You would need 750g (1lb 10oz) to cover a 20cm (8 inch) round cake and 1kg (2¼lb) to cover a 25cm (10 inch) round cake.

Place the trimmed and upturned cake on a cake drum the same size as the cake. Roll a sausage of marzipan and press into the gap that may occur between the edge of the cake and the base board. Also use small amounts of marzipan to fill any holes on the top or sides of the cake.

Brush the cake liberally with the boiled apricot jam. This will help the marzipan stick to the cake and acts as an antiseptic over the cake, but has little flavour and colour so won't affect the overall taste.

Lift the prepared marzipan up and over the top of the cake, keeping it close to the surface, then let the marzipan drape over the cake, allowing the centre to make first contact.

Any excess marzipan trimmings can be added to fresh marzipan and re-worked, as long as they are clean and free from any cake crumb.

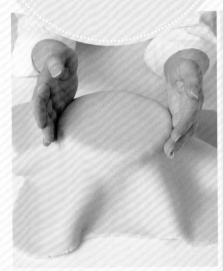

Press into place around the top edge of the cake, where it comes over the side, to protect these edges and prevent cracking. Use one hand to skirt the marzipan out as the other hand brings the marzipan to the cake with a firm upwards brush stroke to stick to the jam and cake. Continue to skirt the marzipan out, and adhere the marzipan to the cake until it is fixed all the way round and you can feel the work surface at the base.

Use a small sharp knife held vertically to trim the excess marzipan from around the base of the cake – leave no more than 2.5cm (1 inch) salvage.

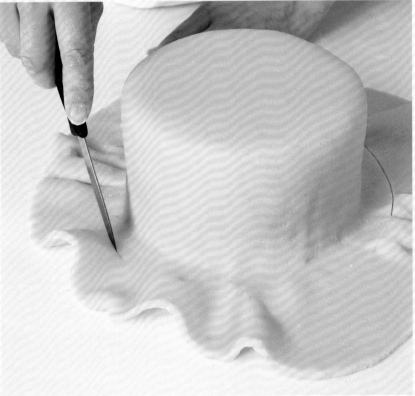

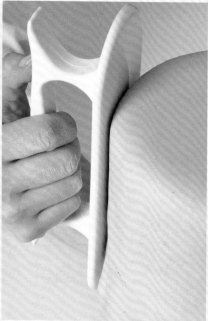

Use the knife to slide underneath the cake and its board, and lift the cake up. Cakes smaller than 20cm (8 inches) can be held on a clawed hand to support the weight of the cake through your whole arm – not on a flat palm with bent wrist. Cakes larger than 25cm (10 inches) can be lifted on to a turntable.

Hold the round edge icing smoother vertically and smooth to bring the marzipan down below the base board until the sides are perpendicular to the top and bottom, straight and even all the way round.

Hold the sharp knife with the blade facing away from you and slice the marzipan cleanly away from beneath the base board as you turn the cake to leave a smooth, clean, professional finish.

Use the straight edge icing smoother to very gently rock around the base cut edge of the marzipan – to gently seal the crumbs – do not be tempted to apply any pressure as you do not want to shape the marzipan at this stage.

Place the cake on a clean working board and hold one of each of the icing smoothers to smooth the top (round edge smoother) and sides (straight edge smoother).

Rub both hands just over the top edge of the cake, working around the cake to bring the top and sides together. The prepared cake is now ready for a top coat of sugar paste (see page 145), royal icing (see pages 152–153) or chocolate (see page 111).

WHAT CAN GO WRONG?

AIR BUBBLES

✳ You have not kneaded the marzipan properly.
Remedy: Either re-knead and roll again, or prick air bubbles with a scribe/pokey tool, ease the air out and rub the marzipan to seal.

CRACKING ON THE EDGES

✳ You have not kneaded long enough, marzipan still too cold.
✳ The marzipan is too thin.
✳ There is too much icing sugar in the marzipan or on the surface.
Remedy: Rub the edges with warm hands.

SIDES NOT STRAIGHT

✳ If it is A-line – the marzipan is too thick or you have not spent long enough smoothing the sides.
Remedy: continue to use icing smoother until the sides are straight.

✳ If it is bulbous – you have used too much buttercream inside the cake.
Remedy: Strip and remove excess buttercream, then re-cover cake.

3 Colouring sugar paste

Sugar paste is available ready made in a spectrum of colours, but for more variety you can blend your own colours to reach a desired shade using edible colour gels. These are concentrated colours and will not dry the paste out. Liquid or dust colours tend not to have enough intensity to colour sugar paste before reaching saturation and either turning the paste sticky or drying it out.

YOU WILL NEED

1 packet of ready-made sugar paste

Edible colour gels of choice

Disposable gloves

MICH'S TIPS

1 It is a really good idea to wear disposable gloves to colour sugar paste as the colour gels are concentrated and can stain.

2 Coloured sugar paste tends to dry to a darker colour and certain colours are prone to fading. Cover coloured cakes and boards at the same time to ensure they dry, darken and fade at the same intensity.

Knead the sugar paste until it is soft and pliable. This will make adding the colour easier. Wearing disposable gloves, dip a cocktail stick in the edible concentrated colour gel and draw this across the surface of the sugar paste. Start with less, as you can always add more. Begin kneading the sugar paste in exactly the same way as you would for marzipan (see page 136). Do not be tempted to use icing sugar at this stage as this will dry the paste out.

Continue to knead using only the top flat part of your hand to avoid making the paste too sticky. Work with purpose to avoid drying the paste and to work the colour through the paste effectively. Cut the ball of paste in half to check the colour has been evenly distributed. Continue if necessary until the colour is even.

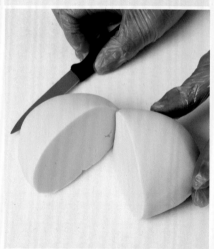

Storage: Wrap any excess sugar paste in a polythene bag to avoid the edges becoming crusty and the paste fading in colour. It will keep for up to 3 months.

4 Covering a cake with sugar paste

Sugar paste is a ready-to-roll icing made from icing sugar, glucose, vegetable oil and gum. It has a similar calorific content to marzipan, creating a wonderful medium for further hand piping, hand painting and decoration. Sugar paste will skin over as it comes into contact with air, forming a firm crust that can be easily cut with a knife without splintering or crushing.

To cover a 15cm (6 inch) round cake

INGREDIENTS

500g (1lb 2oz) sugar paste

Cakes should be covered with marzipan before the top coat of sugar paste is added. A cake covered with marzipan can be covered with sugar paste straight away or left to firm up overnight.

Prepare the sugar paste as per marzipan on page 136. Brush the cake with brandy, vodka or cooled boiled water. This will help the icing to stick to the cake, acts as an antiseptic over the cake and has little flavour and colour. Lift the icing up and over the top of the cake, keeping it close to the surface, then let the icing drape over the cake, allowing the centre to make first contact.

Smooth and shape the icing with rounded and square-edge smoothers as per the marzipan technique on pages 142–143. Leave the prepared cake to dry out and firm up overnight before adding further decoration.

COVERING INDIVIDUAL CAKES

Perfectly decorated and presented individual cakes can be the height of sophistication and skill to showcase your cake decorating. A cake for one makes a perfect present – especially boxed, ribboned, labelled and presented at a celebration or social gathering. Cut the cakes from one larger baked, chilled cake using an individual round cutter or a serrated knife and ruler for square cakes. This way the cakes will be moist through the cake. Anything smaller than 10cm (4 inches) in diameter should be cut from one larger cake. Chilling the cake makes the individual cakes easier to cut out.

COVERING INDIVIDUAL ROUND 5CM (2 INCH) CAKES

Brush the cakes with sieved and boiled apricot jam. Roll out a sheet of icing to 4mm (¼ inch) thick. Use a pizza rotary wheel to cut the sugar paste into small squares large enough to cover the top and sides of the individual cakes (see Note below). Lift and place the sugar paste over the top and sides of the cake.

Cup the paste with your hands to smooth and shape to the base. Use a cutter 1cm (¾ inch) larger than the cake to cut out the paste. Place it over the top of the cake and press down firmly to cut through the icing.

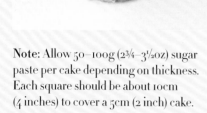

Note: Allow 50–100g (2¾–3½oz) sugar paste per cake depending on thickness. Each square should be about 10cm (4 inches) to cover a 5cm (2 inch) cake.

"These small covered cakes are time-consuming, require skill and patience but will certainly impress the recipient."

Remove the excess paste from around the cake. Use two straight edge smoothers with a forwards and backwards smoothing action to shape, smooth and neaten the sides of the cake. Press the top of the cake to flatten and level. The prepared cake is now ready for further decoration. Leave the cake to firm before fixing ribbon around the base.

For a flawless finish, cover the cakes with a base layer of marzipan and then repeat the process with sugar paste.

COVERING INDIVIDUAL SQUARE CAKES

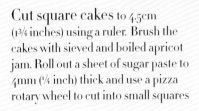

Cut square cakes to 4.5cm (1¾ inches) using a ruler. Brush the cakes with sieved and boiled apricot jam. Roll out a sheet of sugar paste to 4mm (¼ inch) thick and use a pizza rotary wheel to cut into small squares large enough to cover the top and sides of the individual cakes. Lift and place the sugar paste over the top and sides of the cake. Press two straight edge smoothers on opposite sides of the cake to straighten and neaten. Repeat on the remaining two sides. Use a sharp knife to trim straight and as close to the base as possible. The prepared cake is now ready for further decoration. Leave the cake to firm before fixing ribbon around the base.

5 Lining a board with sugar paste & ribbon

Lining a cake drum with sugar paste gives a professional finish to any decorated cake. The board can be covered in the same colour as the cake or a contrasting colour. Individual and shaped cakes can look impressive set on a larger round or square board, lined in a contrasting colour – either glittered, lustred or with a hand-piped message on the board. Boards should be lined at least one day before the cakes are to be placed on them to allow them time to firm and harden so they do not dent or mark. Drums are generally 12mm ($\frac{1}{2}$ inch) thick. Aim to roll the sugar paste to a thickness of 3mm ($\frac{1}{8}$ inch) so a 15mm ($\frac{5}{8}$ inch) ribbon fixed around the side will finish flush with the sugar paste.

COVERING A CAKE BOARD

Brush the surface of the cake drum with cooled, boiled water. Roll a sheet of sugar paste large enough to cover the cake drum, no thicker than 3mm ($\frac{1}{8}$ inch) and smooth the surface with an icing smoother. Lift onto the cake board.

Use an icing smoother to smooth and level the surface once in place. Trim the excess sugar paste to only leave 2cm ($\frac{3}{4}$ inch) salvage around the board.

Lift the board up and hold one hand underneath the cake board, the other holding a small sharp knife vertically with the blade pointing away from you. Start with the knife in contact with the side of the cake board and as you rotate the cake board towards you, slice the knife down through the sugar paste to leave a clean finish. Clean the knife between each slice to prevent icing crumbs on the board. Smooth the edge with a straight edge icing smoother. Leave to firm overnight.

ADDING RIBBON

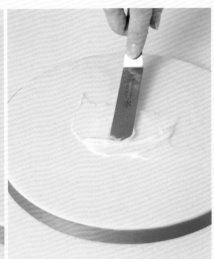

Rub a glue stick around the side of the cake board, then place the board back onto a clean work surface. Fix a length of 15mm (⅝ inch) ribbon around

the base board, making sure the base of the ribbon is flush with the base of the board, not riding up or folding down below. Seal the edges with the glue stick.

Spread a little royal icing in the centre of the lined board. Lift the cake into position. Slide the cake until it is in the correct position either centrally or offset – use a ruler to check.

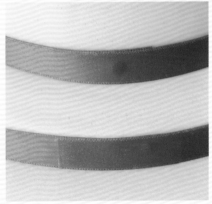

Fix a length of ribbon around the base of the cake to neaten the cake to the board. Dab a little royal icing on the back of the cake and press the ribbon over the icing, making sure the base of the ribbon is flush with the base of the cake. Wind the ribbon around the cake, dab a little royal icing on the back of the initial ribbon and press to seal.

The prepared, ribboned cake is now set on its ribboned, lined board and ready for decoration.

Note: Doubling the base boards by fixing 2 together with glue and adding a thicker (25mm/1 inch) ribbon around the edge creates a more robust, impressive base board.

6 Covering with fondant

Fondant icing is a water glacé icing with added dried glucose powder. Make up the fondant according to the instructions on the packet. It will run smoother if made with warm water, or heated once made. Work to achieve the correct consistency to coat the back of the spoon, before attempting to colour the fondant.

FONDANT ICING

Fondant differs from glacé icing in that the sugar comes ready mixed with additional dried glucose powder. This means the resulting icing is thicker, but has a viscosity that allows it to be poured to cover the tops and sides of cakes for a complete coverage. Glacé icing is generally used as a top frosting only. The fondant is made with freshly boiled water or the fondant is gently warmed before applying to make it cover more easily. At this point the fondant can be coloured or left white. As the fondant cools it will skin over and set firm to touch but still have a soft bite, making it a perfect choice to cover lighter cakes (see page 224). This icing is poured, or the cakes dipped, which makes it a good choice for covering delicate, small, intricate-shaped cakes.

MICH'S TIPS

1 The marzipan helps to protect the fragile crumb of the cake as well as lock in the moisture. It may be necessary to cover the whole cake. In which case roll the marzipan out very thinly – no more than 2mm per cake – then cover, shape and trim with a larger round cutter or a sharp knife.

2 Always make excess fondant. It is relatively inexpensive, yet a large amount is required to smoothly, evenly and professionally cover one small cake!

YOU WILL NEED

Prepared fondant icing

Disposable piping bag

Wire rack

Non-stick baking parchment

Place the prepared cakes on a wire rack set over a sheet of non-stick baking parchment. Fill a piping bag with prepared fondant icing. Pipe the fondant over the top and sides of the cakes to ensure all the corners and sides are covered. Gently tap the wire rack to allow the icing to find its own level and shape and excess to drip off. Leave to set for a minute.

Trim the base of the cake with a sharp knife or small palette knife, then carefully lift the cake off the wire rack and into position for decorating or into foil cases. Leave to dry completely before adding further decoration – this can take up to 2 hours.

Chill the cakes before coating or dipping to firm, stabilize and maintain shape. It can be difficult to achieve a neat finish around the base of fondant-covered cakes this is why they are often presented in foil cases.

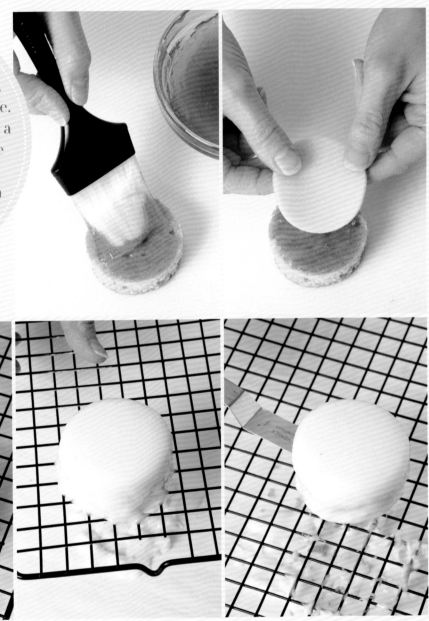

Covering with royal icing

Royal icing is a traditional covering for rich fruit celebration cakes. With its origins in the Victorian era, the super white icing was considered the height of wealth, purity and luxury. Layers of royal icing are built up over several days to ensure a thick, even coat.

INGREDIENTS

1 x 15cm (6 inch) square cake

500g (1lb 2oz) marzipan

1 quantity Royal Icing (see pages 130–131), made with 7 egg whites and glycerine

YOU WILL ALSO NEED

Small sharp knife

Icing scraper

Ruler

Place the trimmed cake upside down in the centre of the presentation cake drum – ideally this should be 5–7cm (2–3 inches) larger than the cake. If necessary, fix in position with a little boiled and sieved apricot jam. Fix a sausage of marzipan into the gap between the base of the cake and the cake board. Trim with a sharp knife to ensure the sides are straight and flush. Also fill in any holes on the top and sides with nuggets of marzipan.

Brush one side of the cake with sieved and boiled apricot jam and fix a 4mm (¼ inch) thick panel of marzipan cut to shape and size. Repeat with all sides and press the joins to seal.

Brush the top of the cake with jam. Roll and cut a square of marzipan 4mm (¼ inch) thick to fit the top of the cake. Use two straight edge smoothers held at right angles to neaten and sharpen the sides. Leave to dry out and firm overnight.

MICH'S TIPS

1 Royal icing is absorbent; other strong colours will bleed into the icing.

2 Royal icing is time-consuming to apply – typically 3 days to allow all the coats to dry.

3 Cover a faux polystyrene tier in place of a soft cake ahead of time and bake the fresh cake the day before the event. Royal ice the top only and serve directly from the kitchen.

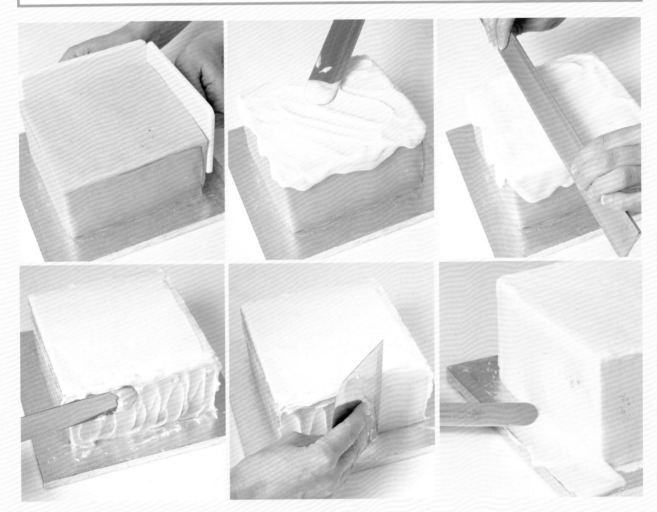

Paddle the royal icing with a palette knife on a clean work surface to remove air bubbles before lathering the top of the cake. Using an icing blade held at a 45-degree angle, drag it across the surface of the icing. It may take a few attempts to achieve a smooth, level finish. Trim the excess icing from the sides of the cake using a sharp knife and leave to firm and set for at least 4 hours.

Work on the 2 opposite side panels first. Lather the freshly made royal icing onto the two opposite sides. Use a side scraper to draw the icing towards you to achieve a smooth, straight finish. Neaten the top and edges with a sharp knife. Leave to firm and set before icing the remaining 2 opposite sides. Repeat the entire process for the top and sides a maximum of 3 times to achieve a firm, even, stable finish.

Finish by smoothing royal icing on the base board/cake drum with a small round-bladed palette knife and neaten. Leave to dry overnight before decorating.

Storage: Store excess royal icing in a sealed, clean container and use within 7 days. Mix without beating to avoid adding air bubbles before each use.

8 Central stacking

Stacking tiers is an impressive way to showcase cakes. Tiers of different flavours can be incorporated in one design and the result is impressive. The base tier should always be the heavier cake to allow for the softer tiers to be positioned at the top of the cake. All tiers and base boards should be covered and allowed to dry overnight before attempting to be stacked. If the sugar paste has not dried out firmly it will turn very sticky and become unstable when the upper tiers are stacked on top. Dowelling rods are like internal stilts which support the tier above by anchoring it to the tier below.

YOU WILL NEED

1 cake covered in marzipan and sugar
   paste (see pages 136–145)

Dowelling rods – 6 per tier

Pencil and ruler

Heavy-duty scissors and a spirit level

Fix the base tier into position on the base board as shown on page 149. Insert a dowelling rod in the centre of the cake and force down with a twisting/boring motion. This will minimize the damage to the surface of the cake.

Use a pencil to mark the point at which the dowelling rod is flush with the surface of the cake. Place your hand either side of the dowelling rod as shown to support the surface of the cake as you gently withdraw the dowelling rod – again using the twisting movement.

> Only when all dowelling rods are the same length can they be effectively inserted into the cake.

> *"I always place a spirit level on top of each tier once dowelled and stacked to check it is even and do this on every tier to the top of the cake."*

Line the marked dowelling rod against 5 others pressed squarely against a cake board or flat surface. Use a ruler to mark all the dowelling rods at the same marked line with a pencil. Holding the dowelling rod close to the mark, use a pair of heavy-duty scissors to carefully score the line.

Firmly hold both ends of the dowelling rod just either side of the mark and carefully snap the dowelling rod in two. Retain all the lengths that need to be inserted into the cake. Repeat with all the dowelling rods. Stand them up and check at eye level that they are all exactly the same length. Only when all dowelling rods are the same length can they be effectively inserted into the cake.

Place the first dowelling rod back into the previous hole in the centre and ensure it is still flush to the surface of the cake. Insert the remaining dowelling rods in a circle, spaced out around the middle dowel, using the same twisting/boring action and making sure they sit within the diameter of the tier to be placed on top. Some may be just below the surface, some may be protruding slightly – this is all okay as the tier will sit level on these stilts when it is iced into position.

Spread a little royal icing on the surface. Lift the upper tier into position. View the cake from all angles to ensure it is sitting centrally over the lower tier. Fix a length of ribbon around the base of the tier.

MICH'S TIPS

1 If there is a large gap between the tiers, fill with royal icing of the same colour from a piping bag (with no nozzle – but cut to fit) to act as a filler. Leave to dry before fixing the ribbon in place.

2 When checking your cut dowels, if one is too long, trim with heavy-duty scissors until it is the right length. If it is too short, discard it and cut a fresh dowel.

9 Off-centre stacking

Off-centre stacking can be an effective way to present a two-tier cake that does not make it look like it is missing a third tier. It allows for the decoration to cascade down the front of the cake, or for a message to be hand piped on the base board or base tier. The principles are the same as for central stacking; remember to dowel further towards the back of the cake, but not too close to the edge or the cake will be unstable.

INGREDIENTS

2 different-sized round cakes covered in marzipan and sugar paste (see pages 136–145)

1 base board, 8cm (3 inches) bigger than the diameter of the largest tier

YOU WILL ALSO NEED

Dowelling rods – 4–8 per tier

Pencil and ruler

Heavy-duty scissors and a spirit level

Fix the base tier into position on the base board, offset to the back. Dowel the tier flush to the surface, but positioned towards the back of the cake following the basic instructions on pages 154–155. Spread a little royal icing over the dowelling rods and lift the upper tier into position. Once the tiers are securely in position, seal the base of the tier with a length of ribbon.

This method will ensure that an uneven lower tier can still support a level upper tier.

"I keep any cut or discarded lengths of dowelling rods to use to add coloured gels to royal icing, sugar paste or buttercream."

10 Using pillars

Pillars add great height between tiers, but care should be taken to ensure they are level and evenly spaced. Cakes covered with royal icing are very strong and it is not necessary to dowel the upper tiers if they are small and relatively light. Tiers covered with sugar paste should always have dowelling rods inside their pillars to support the upper tiers.

To ensure upper tiers are level, view the cake from the front and side. If the tier needs to move, lift it in short, sharp movements and set it down rather than sliding or dragging the tier which would dislodge the pillars.

Place a small round or square drum into position on the lower tier to be dowelled for pillars. Mark the pillars into position around the cake board. These can be iced directly into position with royal icing or marked for dowelling rods if they are to have additional support (see instructions for inserting dowelling rods on pages 154–155). Remove the central cake board and place the upper tier into position (in situ, on location). Use a spirit level to check the tiers are even.

"It is always a good idea to ice pillars into position for stability."

11 Blocking

An effective way to add height and stature to cakes while retaining stability is blocking, either with fresh or sugar flowers and ribbons. Dowelling rods separate and support the tiers but a disc or square block of polystyrene within the dowelling rods increases the surface area, ensuring the cake is even and stable. The wired fresh or sugar flowers and ribbons can then be inserted into the polystyrene block. The usual separation is 2.5cm (1 inch) for smaller flowers, 5cm (2 inches) for a single row of roses or 7.5cm (3 inches) for a double row of flowers, but you could go higher.

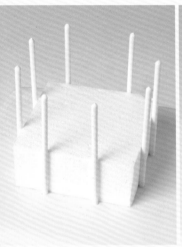   

YOU WILL NEED

Dowelling rods – 8 per tier

Polystyrene block 5cm (2 inches) smaller than the base diameter of the upper tier (cake or board, whichever is the larger)

Heavy-duty scissors

Pencil

Place the polystyrene block on the surface of the lower tier, measured to be central either by eye or using a ruler. Butt dowelling rods up to the polystyrene and insert them around the polystyrene to anchor it by twisting them downwards into the base tier.

Mark the point at which the dowel is flush with the surface of the polystyrene block with a pencil. Remove the polystyrene block and set to one side. Carefully remove the dowels one by one – again twisting them as you withdraw them from the cake.

MICH'S TIPS

1 It is imperative that all the dowels are cut to the same length to ensure the upper tier is level. Simply cutting the dowels at the point where they are flush with the polystyrene will result in an uneven and unstable cake.

2 If blocking with fresh flowers it is easier to block the polystyrene before the upper tier is placed into position. Dress all the tiers with flowers first, then simply lift and assemble them into position.

Lay the dowels cake side down, flush against a cake board. Line a ruler up along the marks and find the average line. Draw a darker line across the average line and if necessary add a little vertical line to this mark to ensure the true mark is clear and recognizable. Cut (or score) each dowel and snap it to the desired length. Check the dowels all together at eye level against a firm surface once they are all cut to ensure they are all completely level. Carefully insert the dowels back into the cake and place the polystyrene block in the centre. Lift the upper tier into position making sure it is straight and even from the front, back and sides. Finally, check with a spirit level to ensure the cake is even. The cake is now ready to be dressed between the tiers.

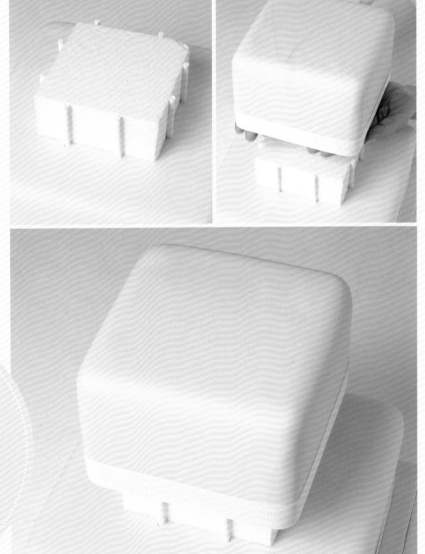

Check the cut dowels at eye level to ensure they are the same length before inserting them into the cake.

Lesson 3

Decorating

* HAND PIPING
* HAND MOULDING
* HAND PAINTING

Hand Piping

Hand piping is a more advanced technique that can be applied directly onto the cake either freehand following a template; or by creating run outs and royal iced components as on the butterflies on pages 242–243, then adhering them to the cake. In this chapter I aim to teach you the fundamentals of hand piping – how to make, fill and hold a piping bag; how to pipe perfect pearls, straight lines and build your confidence with hand-piped messages and pressure piping. Practice makes perfect – and there's no fast track to experience.

1 Making a piping bag

Disposable silicone piping bags are the most effective way of hand piping royal icing, glacé icing and some chocolate detail. They can be easily made once you know how and can be made up in different sizes and stored. Make these from sheets of silicone baking paper or cut them from a roll. They can be used without a nozzle and simply snipped once filled, or used in conjunction with an array of nozzles in numerous shapes and sizes to pipe flowers, stars and scrolls as well as pearls, lines and messages.

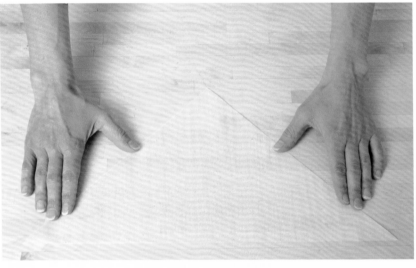
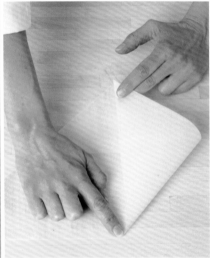

Start with a triangle of silicone baking paper – this should be a right-angled triangle (the two shorter sides the same length). The easiest way is to make a square of paper and fold it in half diagonally. Cut along this fold with a sharp blade to make 2 equal triangles.

Position the triangle on the work surface with the longest side furthest from you – the point facing you. Position one finger along the long edge opposite the point facing you. Bring the left point down to meet the central point facing you. This will form a right angle and a straight line down to the central point.

Turn the left point over so the back of it is in line with the point facing you as it lines up – this will start to create the cone shape.

"I staple the bags for ease and speed as the non-stick silicone bags won't stick with tape."

✗ What not to do
When bringing the points together, if there is a gaping hole at the tip, gently use your thumbs to tease the base of the bag outwards and towards you to close the tip of the piping bag. As long as you start with a right-angled triangle and all the points line up, front, middle and back, the bag will form the perfect tip and cone shape.

Hold the cone at the join of the 2 points. Bring the top right point across the front of the bag and round to line up with the first 2 points – but at the back of the cone. Aim to ensure the cut edges are all vertical and line up with the first point facing you. Staple the back where the 3 points all come together or fold them over to hold and seal. Either fill the bag with icing, or if using a piping nozzle, cut the tip off the piping bag before inserting and filling with icing.

2 Filling a piping bag with royal icing

It may sound basic but learning how to fill a piping bag properly will prevent many wasted piping bags, split bags and icing oozing out from around the nozzle. Make sure the piping bag is made from a right-angled triangle of silicone baking paper for maximum strength and optimum shape.

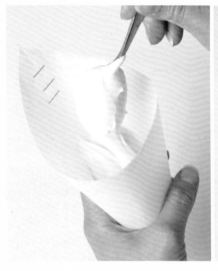  

Hold the piping bag in one hand with the seams and back of the bag facing away. Cut the tip off and insert the piping nozzle if using (if you are not using a nozzle, do not cut the tip off yet). Use a teaspoon to half fill the piping bag with royal icing.

Press your thumb against the piping bag, directly on top of the royal icing so it reaches the back of the piping bag as shown. This will ensure the royal icing is pushed down towards the tip and air is expelled out the sides.

Fold the left side inwards and crease into position. Keep your thumb firmly on the pad of icing inside the bag.

✗ What not to do

While it can look very pretty to just fold the piping bag over at the top once it is filled, the air has not been expelled and there is no control over pressure of the icing. As soon as you start to use this bag, the air will be allowed to move around the bag and the icing nozzle will be able to work its way back up inside the bag, and the icing will ooze out around it.

Fold the right side of the bag in, again ensuring your thumb remains firm on the pad of icing and all the air is expelled through the back of the bag.

Now roll the back of the bag down to the pad of icing, with both sides firmly tucked inside. The filled bag is now ready to use. Snip the end of the piping bag with sharp scissors if not using a nozzle.

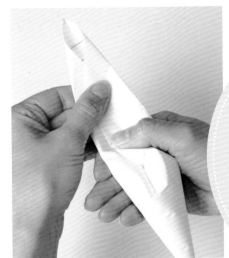

Store filled piping bags inside a sealed polythene bag until you are ready to use them to prevent the icing drying out and the nozzle from clogging up.

3 How to pipe

Learning how to pipe will give you the building blocks to unlock many cake decorating techniques. Whether you are piping pearls, lines, scrolls or messages, some simple, fundamental rules apply. These techniques use royal icing; it is important to understand the different viscosities of royal icing to have the perfect icing.

MICH'S TIPS

1 Always ensure the tip of the nozzle is clean by gently pinching the end with a clean cloth.

2 Be careful to understand your own pressure. The stiffer the icing, the more pressure you will have to apply and the slower you will be able to pipe. The softer the icing, the lower the pressure and the faster the speed. There is no fast track to experience!

3 Royal icing should be stiff but still glossy and mallow. It should have the consistency of freshly whipped double cream. Too runny and the piped decoration will not hold its shape. Too stiff and the hand-piped decoration will be brittle and likely to break.

4 Make a series of piping bags – more than you think you will need – ahead of tackling a hand-piping project.

5 Check nozzles are scrupulously clean and free of other coloured icing before inserting in a piping bag and filling with fresh icing. Store filled piping bags inside a sealed polythene bag to prevent the tips drying out. Royal icing can be kept in an airtight container for up to 7 days, but stir well before using. Over time the icing will thin as the air is lost and the egg white ages.

Piping bags should be held in the hand with which you write. Hold the tip between your first and second finger, with your thumb firmly on the back or base of the piping bag. Always pipe with two hands, using your non-piping hand to help guide you. Icing is forced out of a nozzle/piping bag by extrusion (applying pressure to force icing out as the bag is pulled towards you).

It is important to always touch the tip down at the beginning and end of a moving direction, such as lines or messages, but otherwise always pull the tip away to allow the icing to fall into position.

Once mastered, coloured icing can be used to decorate cakes with columns of royal iced pearls.

Don't squeeze the piping bag with your fingers. Your thumb applies the pressure – the fingers are used for direction.

Tutorial Perfect pearls

The perfect iced pearl can seem the simplest of all hand-piped decoration, yet it can be one of the hardest to master. Use my top tips below to practise and perfect your technique. For this cake I have used royal icing made with unrefined icing sugar (see pages 130–133). It has a natural caramelized colour and flavour.

Cover a cake the day before decorating to ensure it has firmed, set and dried. Place a template against the cake and prick the design onto the cake using a pokey tool.

Fill a piping bag with No. 1.5 nozzle and royal icing. Place the nozzle against the first point marked and apply pressure with your thumb. Pull the nozzle towards you and away from the

cake to let the icing flow. Release the pressure as you attach the loop back to the next marker point. Repeat. Pipe a second row of loops, dropping them lower than the first line.

Pipe a single larger pearl at the top of each garland to seal the points.

Pipe smaller pearls inside the garland loops around the cake.

Finish with a vertical line of 3 smaller pearls, culminating in a single larger pearl.

MICH'S TIPS

1 Use the correct size nozzle for the size of pearl you wish to pipe. Too large and the pearl will not have a rounded spherical shape. Too small and it will take a long time to pipe each pearl.

2 Ensure your nozzle is angled at exactly 90 degrees to the cake – this way the icing will hit the cake and form a perfect circular base. If the nozzle is at an angle as you apply pressure, the icing will be forced in one direction creating an uneven pearl.

3 The nozzle should be held just away from the cake as you apply pressure. This allows the icing to extrude from the nozzle and leave the perfect circular base to the pearl. Too close and the nozzle will be touching the cake and the icing will have to be forced out and behind the nozzle creating an uneven pearl. Too far away from the cake and the icing will drop due to gravity before touching the cake.

4 Once the nozzle is in position at the correct angle and you start applying pressure, do not move the nozzle until you have built up the size and shape of the desired pearl. Then, and only then, release the pressure and snatch the nozzle away. There is a real temptation to bring the nozzle towards you as you start piping – DON'T!

✗ What not to do

Icing is extruded out of the nozzle – this means it is forced out under pressure and the nozzle must always be pulled towards never pushed away to work with the forces of physics – not against them.

Often I see the mistake of not pulling the nozzle away from the cake when piping loops, lines and scrolls – resulting in a pressure piped line which can be uneven and bumpy.

Pulling the nozzle towards you when piping a pearl results in cones and peaks on the pearl rather than a perfect spherical pearl.

Tutorial Vertical lines

This candy stripe design is one of our iconic decorating techniques: hand piping parallel vertical lines with a minimum of three contrasting colours to create a striking design. I have decorated an individual cake here, but you can apply the same technique to larger cakes.

Have all colours made up and ready in their piping bags before you start piping. The royal icing for piping lines can afford to be slightly slacker to adhere better to the cake and avoid air bubbles in the stripes. Make contact at the tip of the cake then draw the nozzle away to allow the line to fall into position – this will keep the perfect shape and help you keep a straight line.

When piping the first line keep the tip parallel with the icing so it can be 'pushed' against the cake to adhere. Repeat these lines around the cake at 2cm (¾ inch) intervals. Repeat for the second and third colours to fill the space, finishing with a pearl at the base of each line. Pipe 3 green leaves on the top (see page 114) and place the rose in position. Leave to firm overnight.

WHAT CAN GO WRONG?

WIGGLY LINES
☀ Piping bag is held too close.
☀ Applying too much pressure.
☀ Not piping fast enough.
Remedy: Pull the bag away once contact has been made, apply less pressure and maintain even speed.

BROKEN LINES
☀ Piping too fast.
☀ Not enough pressure.
☀ Not maintaining right angle.
Remedy: Hold a knife vertically and carefully remove the broken line. When piping, slow down and apply more pressure.

INGREDIENTS

1 x 5cm (2 inch) round cake covered in green sugar paste (see page 144)

Royal icing, coloured in 3 shades (see pages 130–132)

Green royal icing (see page 132)

1 x Hand-moulded Rose in yellow sugar paste (see pages 196–198)

YOU WILL ALSO NEED

3 piping bags fitted with No. 3 nozzles

1 piping bag fitted with No. 69 leaf nozzle

Turntable

MICH'S TIPS

1 This technique works well on round cakes that have been covered with sugar paste. This design is not suitable for a square cake as the top corners cross over.

2 Practise piping this technique on an upturned cake tin until you have mastered the design.

This crown cake has been decorated with my monochrome lace design. This is an iconic Little Venice Cake Company design and has been recreated for many weddings, celebrations and retailed through Harrods, Fortnum & Mason and Harvey Nichols. Originally black on white, this design works incredibly well in any choice of two colours.

INGREDIENTS

1 individual cake covered in lime green sugar paste (see page 144)

2–3 teaspoons yellow royal icing per cake (see pages 130–132)

YOU WILL ALSO NEED

20cm (8 inches) of 6cm (2½ inch) ribbon the same colour as your royal icing for the base of the cake

Flower stamp/cutter (or follow the template on page 260 as a guide)

Scribe/pokey tool Turntable

Piping bag fitted with a No. 1.5 nozzle

Fix a length of ribbon around the base of the cake and place it on a turntable. Press a small flower cutter or stamp into the top of the cake to create a template of a flower.

Mark the top edge of the cake with 6 even points using a scribe/pokey tool.

Fill the piping bag with yellow royal icing and pipe the outline of the flower, keeping the nozzle fairly close to the surface of the cake.

Pipe a pearl inside each petal then 3 pearls spreading outwards in a straight line from the base of each petal.

Join the 6 marks around the top edge with a single hand-piped scallop line. The nozzle should make contact with the cake at the beginning and end of each point, but be pulled away from the cake to allow the scallop to form.

MICH'S TIPS

1 Place the cake on a square card to make it easier to move once decorated.

2 If decorating these cakes en masse, pipe all the top flowers and pearls to maintain an even decoration, then pipe the sides of each one in turn.

3 If serving these cakes in two or more flavours, alternate the base and hand-piped colours to identify the flavours.

4 Imprint the flower as soon as the cakes are covered, then leave to set.

Repeat with a slightly deeper scallop line.

Pipe a bow at the top of each scallop. Take the nozzle from the centre out to the top left, vertically down, then diagonally back to the centre. Repeat in the other direction to form the bow.

Pipe the 2 tails of the ribbon beneath the bow.

Pipe a row of 5 tiny evenly spaced pearls beneath the scallop line. Pipe the first in the centre, then 2 either side to be sure of the spacing. Aim to make them all the same size, shape and spacing.

Pipe a second row of 4 pearls between the row above, then continue working downwards to pipe 3, 2 and finish with a single pearl to form a reverse pyramid. Repeat, piping a pyramid beneath each scallop.

Pipe a diamond of pearls above the ribbon, under the ribbon bows. Pipe the top and bottom pearl first, slightly more spaced apart, then the 2 side pearls slightly closer together. Leave the finished cake to dry.

Tutorial Straight lines

This tutorial is intended to build confidence, control and skill with hand piping. Any outline can be used – such as stars or hearts – and the inside filled with a hand-piped trellis. Practise this technique on a lined board or a sheet of paper, before progressing to a covered cake.

INGREDIENTS

1 x 15cm (6 inch) round cake covered with sugar paste (see page 145)

2 tablespoons red royal icing (see page 132)

YOU WILL ALSO NEED

1 x 23cm (9 inch) round cake board lined with white sugar paste (see page 148)

15mm (⅝ inch) red ribbon to edge the board

25mm (1 inch) red ribbon to edge the base of the cake

Heart template (see page 262)

Scribe/pokey tool

Piping bag fitted with No. 1.5 nozzle

Piping bag fitted with No. 2 nozzle

Edge the base of the cake and cake board with the red ribbon and place on a cake stand. Mark the outline of the heart template centrally on the top of the cake using the scribe/pokey tool.

Fill the piping bag fitted with the No. 1.5 nozzle with red royal icing and pipe the first line between two marked points as close to the left hand side of the heart as possible. Pipe parallel lines ensuring you adjust the line to fit inside the marked heart template.

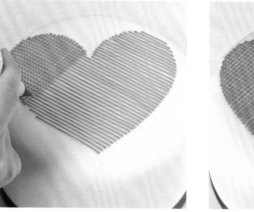

Continue across the full template of the heart. Keep the lines even, straight and parallel. Make sure the nozzle makes contact at the beginning and end of each line, but lifts up and allows the line to fall into place. Fill the heart.

Turn the cake and come back across the heart with a series of parallel lines piped across the first. Care, skill and control will be required here to keep the lines accurate and prevent them from breaking.

Complete the design and breathe! Fill the piping bag fitted with the No. 2 nozzle with red royal icing and finish by piping scallops around the base of the cake marked at 2.5cm (1 inch) intervals. Top each scallop alternately with a pearl and a fleur de lys.

For the best control
don't lift the line too high,
or move to fast. Reduce the
pressure as you bring the
line down to finish at the
right point.

Tutorial Brush embroidery

It can feel quite daunting to pipe free hand onto a covered cake, but can actually be quite liberating! I have taught this cake method in many of my masterclasses and the results never fail to impress. I have chosen to use two contrasting colours to highlight the lace detail on this cake, but this technique works incredibly well using tonal colours – especially if the lace detail itself is highlighted with pearlized lustre.

INGREDIENTS

1 x 15cm (6 inch) round cake covered with sugar paste (see page 145)

3–4 tablespoons white royal icing (see page 130–131)

1 x Hand-moulded Vintage Rose (see page 190), to decorate

YOU WILL ALSO NEED

25mm (1 inch) thick double satin ribbon

3mm (1/8 inch) thick ribbon and a bow

Romantic Lace Veil template (see page 258) or pipe free hand

Scribe/pokey tool

Piping bag fitted with a No. 2 nozzle

Flat-end paintbrush

Edge the base of the cake with the thick ribbon first, then position the thin ribbon above. Finish with a bow.

Use your own vintage lace design, or follow the template on page 258. Prick the design onto the cake with a scribe/pokey tool. Fill the piping bag with white royal icing and pipe the outline of the main flower.

Use a dampened flat-end paintbrush to brush the line inwards and downwards to flatten. The outer edge of the line of hand piping should remain intact to keep a definite edge.

Continue to pipe the other main flowers and brush as before. Pipe a cluster of 5 petal flowers.

Pipe a row of pearls inside the petals of the larger flowers.

Pipe a single pearl inside the small flowers. Hand pipe the stem and leaves. Repeat all over the cake, then leave to dry. Fix the hand-moulded flower in place.

My Little Venice Lace design is iconic and has been used to decorate many celebration and wedding cakes. As a protected trademark it can only be recreated for personal use but the technique of hand piping a repeating symmetrical motif builds skill, confidence and expertise as an introduction to pressure piping.

Trace the Little Venice Lace template (see page 263) onto the side of the cake with a scribe/pokey tool, marking the centre of the pearls and scrolls. Make sure it is positioned above the ribbon, below the height of the cake.

Fit a piping bag with No. 2 nozzle and fill with white royal icing. Keep the template next to you as you begin piping for reference. Start with the outer scrolls and pipe these first to find your rhythm and identify the start and finish of each piece of lace.

Move onto the other scrolls, starting at the top and working down. There are a total of 5, left and right with a central line of symmetry. Ensure the tails of each upper scroll are covered by the head of the lower scroll to keep the design neat.

Start at the back of the cake to find your rhythm; – this way the front will always look perfect and any joins in the design will be concealed at the back of the cake.

MICH'S TIPS

1 Once mastered, you can design your own lace motifs to achieve beautiful, unique designs. Keep the design/template near to you for reference once you actually start to pipe.

2 It will take about 3 pieces of lace to find your rhythm – do not be tempted to scrape off as you will cover the template markings and you will lose your way. Start at the back of the cake and by the time you reach the front, the design will feel more comfortable.

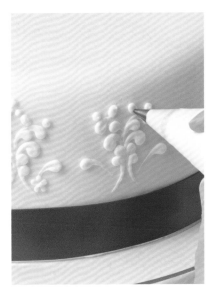

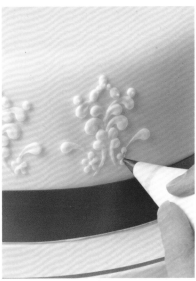

Now the top section of pearls, which are hand piped with angled elongation to create the design. Hand pipe the 2 outer flowers in position by piping 5 tiny pearls flicked into the centre to create a flower. Repeat around the cake.

Tutorial Hand lettering

Hand piping messages directly onto a cake personalizes the cake but can be incredibly daunting if you are inexperienced or lack confidence. Practise these techniques to boost your confidence and control so you never need fear hand piping a message again. The quality of a hand-piped message can make or break an otherwise beautifully decorated cake.

EMBOSSED COLOURED HAND PIPING

Use a ruler and scribe/pokey tool to etch a superfine straight line onto the cake. Print or trace the desired message onto a sheet of tracing paper. Practise on a lined board to build confidence.

Use a non-toxic pencil to draw over the message on the reverse. Carefully position the message, right way up, on the cake and use a pencil to trace it lightly onto the surface of the cake.

Fill a piping bag with a No. 2 nozzle and the same colour royal icing as the covered cake (in this case white). Hand pipe over the traced message. Any mistakes at this stage can be removed with a sharp knife.

Fill a second piping bag with a smaller nozzle (No. 1.5) and coloured royal icing. Simply trace over the message. It is not necessary to wait for the base white coat to dry completely before piping the top message.

MICH'S TIPS

1 It is important to ensure the message is straight – use a ruler and a scribe/pokey tool to etch a superfine line as a guide.

2 Hold the beginning and end of each element of the hand-piped letter to create a small pearl that anchors the letter to the iced cake, rather than snatch the nozzle leaving upward pointing trails of icing.

3 Type the message, font and size on a computer to achieve the correct spacing.

SCROLL COLOURED HAND PIPING

For a larger message, trace the design onto the cake and hand pipe in your chosen colour with a piping bag fitted with a No. 5 star nozzle. Hold the piping bag at an angle rather than vertically over the message to achieve the scroll effect.

BLOCKED RUN OUT LETTERING

Trace the design onto the cake and pipe the outline of each letter with a piping bag fitted with No. 1.5 nozzle and coloured royal icing. Fill a piping bag with coloured flooding icing (see page 133) and flood every other letter. This will allow each letter to skin over and keep its own identity before flooding their adjacent letters to maintain the overall structure and boundaries of each letter.

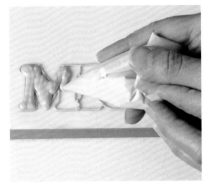

Use a paintbrush to draw the icing into every corner of the letter and remove any air bubbles. Leave to skin over for 30 minutes.

Flood the adjacent letters in the same way and leave to skin over for 30 minutes again.

Fill a piping bag with No. 1.5 nozzle and white or contrasting colour royal icing. Pipe small pearls around each letter to highlight and showcase further decoration.

EMBOSSED ELABORATE HAND PIPING

This is a similar method to the one shown opposite, but using a more elaborate joined-up script. The technique is the same to trace the

message onto the cake; pipe the base layer in a thicker white royal icing, then trace over the top in a thinner coloured

royal icing. This style of font works well for hand piping directly with chocolate, as it flows more readily.

GRANNY'S TIARA

The Girls of Great Britain and Ireland Tiara, affectionately known as 'Granny's Tiara', is part of Queen Elizabeth II's jewel collection. I have designed this cake as a nod to this vintage heirloom. As the tradition of the time would dictate, this cake is entirely decorated with pure white royal icing, separated with plaster of Paris columns and dressed with a single sugar amaryllis.

INGREDIENTS

- 1 x 25cm (10 inch) round cake (10cm/4 inches deep), covered in marzipan and white royal icing (see pages 152–153)
- 1 x 20cm (8 inch) round cake (10cm/4 inches deep), covered in marzipan and white royal icing
- 1 x 15cm (6 inch) round cake (10cm/4 inches deep), covered in marzipan and white royal icing
- White royal icing (see pages 130–133) – 2 quantities with glycerine for covering and 1 quantity without glycerine for decorating
- 1 x Hand-moulded white Amaryllis (see pages 204–205)

YOU WILL ALSO NEED

- 2 x 35cm (14 inch) round double depth base boards lined with white royal icing (see page 153) for the base tier
- 2 x 23cm (9 inch) round double depth base boards lined with white royal icing (see page 153) for the top tier
- 2.5cm (1 inch) bridal white grosgrain ribbon
- Dowelling rods
- Template (see page 262)
- Scribe/pokey tool
- Piping bag fitted with a No. 131 nozzle
- Piping bag fitted with a No. 5 nozzle
- 4 x 7.5cm (3 inch) plaster of Paris pillars
- Extra piping bags

Stack the base two tiers following the instructions on pages 154–155. Edge the doubled base boards with ribbon following the instructions on page 149. Fill the piping bag fitted with the No. 131 nozzle with icing and pipe scrolls around the top and base edge of each tier as shown on page 114. Measure the circumference of each tier using a length of ribbon. Measure the ribbon and divide into 3. Scribe the template onto each tier with the main design centred at each third mark.

Fill the remaining piping bag with icing and start by piping the fleur de lys on the side of the cake as follows: pipe a pearl and draw the nozzle down finishing with a point. Pipe a pearl to the left and draw this across in an arc to the centre and down to finish with a point. Repeat with the right hand side to complete the fleur de lys. Continue to pipe the design further down the symmetrical line, being careful to keep the left and right sides equal.

MICH'S TIPS

1 Extra deep cakes can be achieved by baking more than one cake for each tier and trimming as necessary, or building up a single 7.5cm (3 inch) baked tier with cake boards or a polystyrene base.

2 The design is repeated 3 times around each tier. There will be more space between the design on the larger tiers which can be filled in with additional hand-piped fleur de lys decorations.

Pipe the scroll design either side of the main design, taking care to ensure the head of each scroll covers the tail of the preceding scroll to keep it neat. Pipe a fleur de lys decoration over the final tails of the scrolls as they draw back to the centre. Repeat on all 3 tiers. Leave to dry.

To assemble, position the pillars as shown on page 157 and fix (use dowelling rods inside the pillars if the cake is being covered in sugar paste rather than royal icing). Place the top tier in position. Dress with the sugar amaryllis.

CHANDELIER CAKE

These vintage chandelier silhouettes translate so well when they are hand painted and piped in black detail onto a deep white cake. I have edged the cake in black double satin ribbon and finished with a sumptuous velvet bow. Presenting the cake on a black cake stand completes the chic setting.

INGREDIENTS

1 x 25cm (10 inch) double depth cake covered in white sugar paste (see page 145)

1 x 15cm (6 inch) double depth cake covered in white sugar paste (see page 145)

1 teaspoon black colour dust

½ teaspoon cocoa butter

2 teaspoons black royal icing (see page 132)

YOU WILL ALSO NEED

3m (10ft) of 2.5cm (1 inch) black double satin ribbon

3m (10ft) of 32mm (1¼ inch)white grosgrain ribbon

Cake stand

Chandelier template (see page 261)

Scribe/pokey tool

A selection of paintbrushes

Piping bag fitted with No. 1.5 nozzle

Black velvet bow (allow about 1.5m/5ft)

Note: Choose a cake with firm support and structure – a vanilla cake, chocolate torte or coconut cake would work well.

Stack the cakes centrally (see pages 154–155) and edge the base of each tier with the black and white ribbon. Trace the chandelier template onto the cake using the scribe/pokey tool at strategic positions.

Mix the black colour dust with the cocoa butter in a small bowl. Work from the top down to avoid smudging the detail. Paint the base background of the chandelier in black, then leave to dry for 30 minutes.

Fill the piping bag with black royal icing and hand pipe the pearl strands of the chandelier in position – keep the pearls the same size, same shape and evenly spaced. Add more strands of crystal pearls in black royal icing to create the refined detail. Add the pearl drop crystals by piping a pearl and elongating the nozzle within the pearl.

Pipe the candles and flames into position. Finish by securing a black velvet bow into position on the top tier with icing.

> *"This cake is perfect for a sweet sixteen, 18th, 21st or 30th birthday or a wedding anniversary."*

DAISY QUILT

This design combines hand-piped pearls and pearl drops to create a textured quilt design that has been repeated on all sides of a two-tier cake. By piping all the details in white on a white cake the design has real textural depth and appeal. Change the colours for a more modern, fun approach.

Position the base tier centrally on the base board and line both tiers with grosgrain ribbon. Mark the template against the cake, being sure to take into account the height of the tier and the depth of the ribbon around the base.

Fill the bag with white royal icing. Begin with the vertical and horizontal pearl drops to form a cross. Pipe a pearl, then carefully drag the nozzle to the centre, easing the pressure as you pull. Work inwards. Pipe the 4 diagonal pearls with slightly less pressure so they are smaller than the initial cross.

Pipe the diagonal line of pearls into position making sure they are all the same shape, size and evenly spaced.

Finish each daisy with a larger pearl in the centre to neaten.

INGREDIENTS

1 x 25cm (10 inch) square cake covered in marzipan and sugar paste (see pages 140–145) for the base tier

1 x 15cm (6 inch) square cake covered in marzipan and sugar paste (see pages 140–145) for the top tier

400g (14oz) sugar paste, for blocking

White royal icing (see pages 130–131)

YOU WILL ALSO NEED

1 x 32cm (13 inch) square cake board lined in white sugar paste and edged with 15mm ($^5/_8$ inch) white grosgrain ribbon

2m (6½ft) of 2.5cm (1 inch) white grosgrain ribbon for the base tier

Daisy template (see page 263)

Scribe/pokey tool

Piping bag fitted with No. 2 nozzle

1 x 10cm (4 inch), 2.5cm (1 inch) deep, square polystyrene block

8 dowelling rods

FOR THE TOP ARRANGEMENT

Various ribbon loops (see pages 244–245): 3 x 2.5cm (1 inch) cream grosgrain ribbon loops; 3 x 2.5cm (1 inch) white grosgrain ribbon loops; 3 x 15mm ($^5/_8$ inch) cream grosgrain ribbon loops; 3 x 15mm ($^5/_8$ inch) white organza ribbon loops; and 6 x 15mm ($^5/_8$ inch) white double satin ribbon loops

3 x Vintage Roses (see page 190)

FOR THE BLOCKING

Various ribbon loops (see pages 244–245): 6 x 15mm ($^5/_8$ inch) white double satin ribbon loops; 6 x 2.5cm (1 inch) cream grosgrain ribbon loops; 6 x 25mm white grosgrain ribbon loops; and 6 x 15mm $^5/_8$ inch) white organza ribbon loops

8 x Vintage Roses (see page 190)

TO MAKE THE HAND-MOULDED VINTAGE ROSE

INGREDIENTS

Allow 30–40g (1¼–1½oz) petal paste
per rose

Sugar glue

Ivory royal icing (see pages 130–132)

YOU WILL ALSO NEED

Different sized 5-petal cutters – 3.5cm
(1⅓ inch), 6cm (2½ inch) and 10.5cm
(4 inch)

Small rolling pin

Ball tool

Foam pad or modelling mat

Piping bag fitted with a No. 2 nozzle

Note: Make the inner petals first and
set these in a paint palette to firm. Then
make the outer petals and leave to firm
in a foil tray. By the time you make the
middle layer, the outer and inner petals
will have firmed enough to glue the 3
layers together straightaway. Then leave
the finished flower to firm overnight in
the foil trays.

Knead the petal paste until
smooth and pliable. Roll out to a depth
of about 1–2mm (just under ⅛ inch). Cut
out a 5-petal flower with all 3 different
sized cutters. Place the flowers on the
foam pad or modelling mat and use the
ball tool to frill the petals. Leave each
layer of petals to dry in a paint palette or
foil cup for at least 1 hour or until they

are dry and firm. Fix the 3 layers together
using royal icing or sugar glue to hold
them in position.

Fill the piping bag with ivory royal
icing and pipe a pearl of icing into the
centre of the flower followed by a ring of
smaller pearls.

TO MAKE THE TOP ARRANGEMENT

Knead and shape a golf ball-sized
piece of sugar paste and dome it slightly.
Trim all the ribbon bow wires for this
top arrangement to a maximum length
of 2.5cm (1 inch) using heavy-duty
scissors. Insert the 3 x 2.5cm (1 inch)
cream grosgrain at the base of the sugar-
paste dome, in a triangle position, tails
facing downwards.

Place the 3 x 2.5cm (1 inch) white
grosgrain directly above the first 3
ribbons.

Insert the 3 x 15mm (⅝ inch) cream
grosgrain ribbon loops directly above
these to form a pyramid.

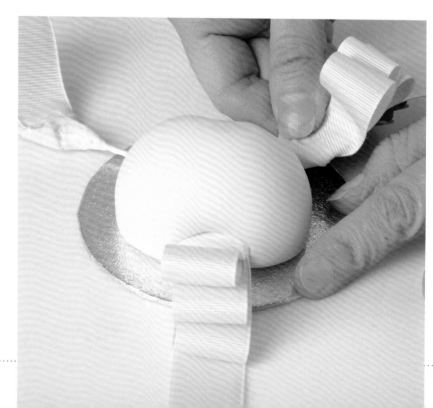

Insert the 3 x 15mm (5/8 inch) white organza loops at the very top in the centre in between the 15mm (5/8 inch) cream grosgrain. Insert the 6 x 15mm (5/8 inch) white double satin loops either side of the initial 2.5cm (1 inch) cream grosgrain ribbons.

Trim all the tails by holding taut and snipping with sharp scissors at an acute angle.

Lift this ribbon skeleton into position onto the top tier, held in place with a little water. Pipe 1/2 teaspoon of royal icing onto the back of 3 vintage flowers and position these into the 3 spaces framed by the ribbons.

Press the centres of the 3 flowers at the same time to tighten and neaten the top arrangement. The centre of the flower is the most stable, least fragile point to press.

TO BLOCK THE BASE TIER

Dowel and block the cake as show on pages 158–159. Dampen the surface of the cake around the polystyrene block.

Knead and roll a sausage of sugar paste 2.5cm (1 inch) thick to fit all the way around, snug up against the polystyrene block.

Place the top tier in position, making sure it is level and straight from all angles.

Pipe ½ teaspoon of royal icing onto the back and base of a vintage flower and set this in position on the corner of the base tier, making sure the flower is anchored to the base tier and the sausage of sugar paste between the tiers.

For added stability, ice the top tier into position on the polystyrene block and transport as one complete tiered, stacked cake.

MICH'S TIP

If you are making a number of the hand-moulded vintage flowers, make all the smaller layers first and leave these to dry in a paint palette with wells. Move on to making all the outer petals and set these in foil cups to firm. By the time you finish with the middle layers the outer and inner layers will be dry enough for you to fix the middle layers straight into position as they are made, finished with the inner layers and you will be able to press them all together without the middle and inner layers shattering.

Choose 3 ribbon loops and twist the wires together to make one strong wire. Trim the length with heavy-duty scissors to 4cm (1½ inches) and insert this up against the vintage rose, pushing the wire into the sugar paste sausage. Fix the next vintage flower up against these ribbons and repeat around the cake until it is blocked and all the gaps are filled. Trim the ribbon loop tails so they are short and spiky. Leave the royal icing to set.

Hand Moulding

Hand moulding or using cutters is a good introduction to **decorating** cakes as you will make all the components before placing them onto the cake. This builds **confidence** and allows you to manage your time effectively. You can be sure you are **happy** with all the **elements** before positioning them on the cake. These techniques include **models, flowers** and **shapes**. **Decorations** can be made up to 3 months in advance and stored in cake boxes. Avoid sealed or airtight containers as any **moisture** inside will cause the decorations to mould and crumble.

Tutorial Chocolate roses

This is the simplest and fastest method I have found for making beautiful roses in chocolate, sugar paste or gum paste to decorate cakes, cupcakes, crown cakes and cookies. Very few utensils are required and you can make these up to 3 months in advance and store them in a cake box.

INGREDIENTS

Allow 20g (¾oz) chocolate (or other coloured) sugar paste per rose

YOU WILL ALSO NEED

Sharp knife

An A4 document pouch slit open on 3 sides

Roll a sausage of chocolate sugar paste to a thickness of 2.5cm (1 inch) and cut off the rounded end.

Cut 6 even discs of chocolate each 2–3mm (⅛ inch) thick – naturally the edge in contact with the work surface will become flatter and less rounded.

Place these discs inside a plastic pouch all facing the same direction, which will allow for each one to be smoothed and shaped without sticking.

Press each petal lightly with the base of your hand to begin the smoothing and rounding process.

Use your thumb to smooth the rounded side of the petal only – leave the straight edge that was in contact with the work surface completely untouched.

Open the pouch and rub the first petal from the fatter straight edge to remove it off the sheet and put a natural curl in the petal.

Turn the petal over so the completely flat shiny side that was face down is now face up, curling away over your finger. Curl this first petal up, tightly and closely, to create the centre of the rose.

Peel the second petal off the sheet. Turn it over so it is curling out. Place the curled centre of the rose seam side down onto the second petal, ensuring it is halfway down the petal. Wrap and pinch the petal around the centre to seal.

Use your finger to curl the top edge of the petal down and under to shape the rose.

Add the third petal on the opposite side to the second and repeat the pinching and shaping.

Make a selection of roses and buds in different sizes for authenticity and versatility.

Place the base of the rose between your two first fingers supported in your hands. Gently rub the base of the rose backwards and forwards to shape the base of the rose.

Add the final 3 petals in one layer around the rose, fixing one side into position but leaving the other side open to tuck the next petal inside.

Once all 3 petals are in position, press to seal and close and then shape each petal to create the rose shape.

Trim the base off the rose using a sharp knife with the blade held away. Move to a clean cake board to allow the rose to firm up overnight.

Chocolate roses can be lustered with gold spray or gilded with gold leaf (see pages 254–255) for an opulent finishing touch.

FOR CHOCOLATE LEAVES

Allow 15g (¾oz) chocolate sugar paste
per 3 leaves

Roll out the sugar paste to a depth
of 2mm (⅛ inch). Use a plunger cutter
to vein and cut out various sizes of rose
leaves. Give these a simple twist, then
leave them to firm up in these set shapes.

"I balance the lily over a rolling pin to achieve a uniform curl."

FOR CHOCOLATE LILIES

Allow 25g (1oz) modelling chocolate
per lily

YOU WILL ALSO NEED

Rolling pin

Arum lily cutter

Knead the modelling chocolate
until smooth and pliable and roll out
to a thickness of 2–3mm (⅛ inch). Cut
the shape out using a 7cm (2¾ inch)
arum lily cutter. Roll a 5cm (2 inch)
length of modelling chocolate into a
torpedo shape and place inside the lily.
Curl the lily around the torpedo centre
and seal the base of the lily petal. Curl
the tip of the lily down to finish, then
leave to firm overnight.

CHOCOLATE CORNUCOPIA

This cake looks very impressive but all of the components are made beforehand and then decorated once the fresh cakes are baked, covered and stacked. I have gilded the decorated cake with gold lustre spray to highlight the detail. This design can be adapted for individual crown cakes, single tiers or applied as a top decoration to a poured ganache cake.

INGREDIENTS

1 x 35cm (14 inch) round cake board lined with chocolate sugar paste (see page 145)

1 x 25cm (10 inch) round cake covered with chocolate sugar paste (see page 145)

1 x 15cm (6 inch) round cake covered with chocolate sugar paste (see page 145)

500g (1lb 2oz) chocolate sugar paste

Selection of hand-moulded chocolate roses, lilies and leaves (see pages 196–199) – about 10–15 of each rose (varying sizes) and lily and 25 leaves

Melted dark chocolate

Edible gold lustre spray

YOU WILL ALSO NEED

2.5m (8¼ft) of 15mm (¾ inch) brown grosgrain ribbon

Pastry brush

Freeze spray

Note: It is a good idea to make excess roses, leaves and lilies to be able to choose the best fit when creating the cascade. Any extras will keep for up to 3 months.

Stack the cakes off centre as shown on page 156. Surround each tier and board with grosgrain ribbon. Roll the chocolate sugar paste into a sausage about 2.5cm (1 inch) thick. Wind this into position around both tiers of the cake using melted dark chocolate to hold it in place. This will act as the base and support for the cascade of chocolate flowers and leaves. Trim the base.

Starting at the top, brush the first 5–7.5cm (2–3 inches) of the sausage with melted chocolate and fix the first lily in position. Build up the design by adding roses of different sizes either side of the lily, using the sausage of sugar paste and melted dark chocolate to anchor each one. Freeze spray will set the melted chocolate immediately, helping to hold the design firm as you work.

As you reach the side of the cake, anchor the lower roses and lilies into position at the base of the tier so that they are stable, then build the design up rather than trying to balance it coming down. Use leaves and small chocolate rosebuds to fill the smaller gaps. Once the garland is complete, spray just the garland (not the cake) with edible gold lustre.

TRIO OF MINI WEDDING CAKES

These cakes have a refined opulence and nod to Marie Antoinette who was rumoured to have announced 'Let them eat cake!' I think they look very *Pride and Prejudice* – reminiscent of the Bennett girls in their fine frocks. These are quite fiddly to make, but make great table centre decorations or as part of a dessert table.

INGREDIENTS

1 x 7.5cm (3 inch) round cake covered in pastel-coloured sugar paste (see page 145)

1 x 5cm (2 inch) round cake covered in pastel-coloured sugar paste (see page 145)

1 x 4cm (1½ inch) round cake covered in pastel-coloured sugar paste (see page 145)

White royal icing (see page 130)

White pearls

4–5 hand-moulded sugar paste roses (see pages 196–198)

YOU WILL ALSO NEED

1 x 10cm (4 inch) drum board lined with sugar paste

35cm (17 inches) of 15mm (²/₃ inch) cream grosgrain ribbon

Piping bag

Stack the 3 round covered cakes centrally (see pages 154–155). It is acceptable to stack these cakes directly on top of one another without internal boards or dowelling rods as the cakes are so light. Edge the cake board with ribbon and place the stacked cakes on the covered base board.

Working on one tier at a time, pipe a trail of royal icing around the base of the tier. Place a row of sugar pearls into position on top of the piped trail of icing. For the base tier, fix 3 rows of pearls on top of each other, middle tier should have 2 rows of pearls and then just a single row for the top tier.

Dress the cake with hand-moulded sugar roses, held in position with royal icing.

MICH'S TIPS

1 These cakes should be stamped out of one larger cake. Use rich fruit cake or creamed cakes that are more stable and have good support.

2 Pipe pearls rather than applying individual pearls for convenience.

3 Make your own pearls by rolling sugar paste balls and spray with pearl lustre.

4 Make two-tone sugar roses following the technique on pages 208–209 – use a darker colour for the inner petals and a paler colour for the outer petals.

Tutorial Amaryllis flower

These sugar flowers are perfect for winter- or Christmas-themed cakes as they are naturally in season at this time. Made up of 6 petals, they are blousy and full, which creates real impact as a single corsage on celebration cakes. They are time-consuming to make as each petal is wired and must be allowed to dry. They are, however, large and impressive and can be made well in advance to aid preparation. For added authenticity, you could also wire 6 stamens together and insert these into the centre of the amaryllis.

INGREDIENTS

Allow 60g (2oz) white petal paste per flower

YOU WILL ALSO NEED

24-gauge white wire cut into 6 x 15cm (6 inch) lengths

8cm (3¼ inch) amaryllis or arum lily cutter

Foam pad or modelling mat

Ball tool

Veiner

White floristry tape

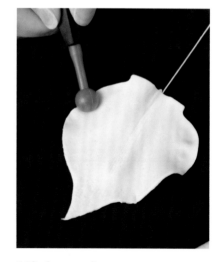

Bend the end of a piece of wire to create a hook. Insert the hook into a large pea-sized ball of petal paste. Twist the petal paste down about 5–6cm (2–2¼ inches) along the length of the wire.

Roll out the petal paste to a depth of 1–2mm (just under ⅛ inch) and cut out the amaryllis shape.

Lift the petal onto the foam pad and shape the edges with a ball tool. For a more authentic finish, follow the next 2 images and add veining to the petal before shaping the edges.

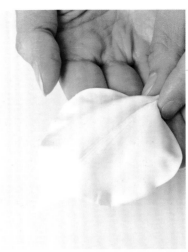

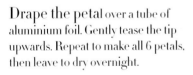

Place the wired paste in the base of a veiner and lift the shaped petal on top. Place the top of the veiner in position and sandwich together. Remove the petal from the veiner – the strengthened wire should be firmly in position at the back now.

Drape the petal over a tube of aluminium foil. Gently tease the tip upwards. Repeat to make all 6 petals, then leave to dry overnight.

When the petals are dry wire the first 3 petals together with floristry tape in a triangle formation. Tape the second batch of 3 petals beneath and between the first 3 petals to make a full and complete amaryllis.

Tutorial Gloriosa lily

Gloriosa lilies or flame lilies have a wonderful vibrancy and delicacy that I have tried to recreate in this sugar version. My aim with making any sugar flower is to be effective but still offer a practical method that ensures these flowers do not take hours to make. As with all sugar flowers, these can be made in advance and stored in a protective box until they are required.

INGREDIENTS

Each flower has 6 petals – allow 30g (1oz) red petal paste per flower

Colour dusts (fuchsia, tangerine and primrose)

YOU WILL ALSO NEED

Mini rolling pin

10cm (4 inch) lily cutter

26-gauge wire cut into 15cm (6 inch) lengths

Veiner

Foam pad or modelling mat

Ball tool

Green floristry tape

Paintbrush

Knead the red petal paste a small amount at a time and roll very thinly on a clean work surface or non-stick workboard, lightly dusted with icing sugar if required to prevent sticking. Use the lily cutter to cut out a lily shape. Thread an elongated ball of paste the size of a large pea onto the end of a hooked wire. Rub the base of the paste down the length of the wire to elongate it and create a bud-like tip. This will add strength and support to each of the petals.

Lay this elongated bud in the centre of the veiner with the clear wire protruding from the end of the veiner. Place the cut-out lily shape on top and place the top of the veiner on the cut-out lily– effectively the lily and wire are sandwiched inside the veiner. Press the veiner very firmly to adhere the wire to the petal and ensure the petal has been marked with the veiner.

"These petals are very delicate. I would suggest making spares that can easily be replaced in case of breakages."

If the paste is very dry or stiff, rub a little white vegetable fat between your thumb and finger before kneading into the paste.

Open up the veiner and check the petal has fixed to the wire and it has been veined. Remove the petal from the veiner and place on a foam pad or modelling mat. Use a ball tool around the outside edges to thin and shape the petal. Lay the petal over a roll of aluminium foil or a rolling pin and allow to dry and firm in position for 4 hours making sure the join of the wire is facing down. Repeat to make 6 petals for each lily.

When the petals are dry, tape the base of each with green floristry tape to strengthen. Dust each petal with fuchsia dust down through the centre and a mixture of orange and yellow around the outside edge. Tape the first petal to the second, petals facing inwards to form a ball. Continue to tape all petals until the gloriosa lily has 6 petals, all facing inwards, and gently tease them into shape.

Tutorial Two-tone flowers

For this technique I have rolled two different colours of petal paste, then layered and rolled them together before cutting out flowers with a 5-petal cutter. When the petals are shaped they have real depth by having one colour on the surface, with another colour beneath showing through. I have used vintage pastel colours here, but this technique also works well with most muted shades.

Knead 2 walnut-sized balls of different coloured petal paste until smooth and pliable. Roll each one out into a long slipper shape, about 1–2mm (just under ⅛ inch) thick. Aim to have both sheets the same size and thickness.

Lay one rolled sheet on top of the other and continue to roll together to an overall thickness of 1-2mm (just under ⅛ inch).

Cut out 5-petal flowers in 3 different sizes.

INGREDIENTS

Allow 30g (1¼oz) petal paste per flower in various colours

Sugar glue

Coloured royal icing, to finish

YOU WILL ALSO NEED

Mini rolling pin

5-petal cutters in varying sizes – 2cm (¾ inch), 3.5cm (1⅓ inch) and 6cm (2½ inch)

Foam pad or modelling mat

Piping bag fitted with a No. 1.5 nozzle

Ball tool

MICH'S TIPS

1 Work on a small amount of paste at a time – it dries out very quickly.

2 Once the coloured pastes are thinly rolled out together, cut some shapes out and then turn them upside down to cut out the opposite colour.

3 Once the pastes have been rolled out together, any offcuts cannot be re-used as the colours will now be blended.

4 Remember to store sugar decorations in a protective box and not an airtight container to avoid them becoming mouldy and crumbling.

Allow the shaped petals to dry and firm placed in a paint palette or foil tray. Fix the three layers with sugar glue or royal icing.

Place the flowers on a foam pad and use the ball tool to shape the petals on each individual flower.

Lay the smaller petals in the well of a paint palette or similar vessel to firm and shape and leave for 2 hours. Larger petals can be laid inside a small bowl or held in position inside a cup made of aluminium foil.

When the petals have firmed, glue the 3 layers together with sugar glue or a dab of royal icing.

Leave the flower to firm and dry completely (overnight or for at least 4 hours), then remove the support.

Fill the piping bag with coloured royal icing and pipe a ring of pearls in the centre of the flower to finish.

MARILYN CAKE

This vintage design adopts muted shades of two-tone roses positioned around the base of a stacked cake. Champagne pearls are delicately hand piped once the roses are in position to add a breathtaking professional finish. This cake has no lined board so position on a cake stand before decorating. Alternatively, line a board 7.5 cm (3 inches) larger than the base tier.

INGREDIENTS

- 1 x 25cm (10 inch) round cake, covered with marzipan and sugar paste (see pages 140–145)
- 1 x 15cm (6 inch) round cake, covered with marzipan and sugar paste (see pages 140–145)
- 27–30 Two-Tone Flowers (see pages 208–209) in various colours
- Cream royal icing (see pages 130–133)

YOU WILL ALSO NEED

- 2.5cm (1 inch) cream grosgrain ribbon
- Cake stand
- Piping bag fitted with a No. 2 nozzle

Stack the cake following the instructions on pages 154–155 and edge the base of each tier with the cream grosgrain ribbon. Place on a decorative cake stand.

Fix the roses into position around the base of each tier, so they all nudge up next to one another and sit flush with the base of the tier.

Fill the piping bag with the cream royal icing and pipe random pearls around the flowers, above the ribbon.

Pipe the pearls once the flowers are in position for a professional finish. Pearls can be piped in a palette of colours to complement the flowers.

Tutorial Hellebore rose

These little hellebores were inspired by a Mother's Day gift from my boys. I have started with a simple 5-petal cutter, but with clever shaping, dusting and piping created a realistic hellebore that can be used to decorate many celebration cakes and individual crown cakes. They are delicate because they only have a single layer of petals so handle them with care.

INGREDIENTS

15g (¾oz) white petal paste per flower

Colour dusts (yellow and green)

White royal icing (see pages 130–133)

Yellow sugar paste (see page 144)

Yellow royal icing (see pages 130–133)

YOU WILL ALSO NEED

Mini rolling pin

6cm (2½ inch) 5-petal cutter

Veiner

Foam pad or modelling mat

Ball tool

Bun tray or paint palette for shaping/
    setting

Paintbrush

2 piping bags fitted with No. 1.5 nozzles

Scribe/pokey tool

Knead the petal paste until smooth and pliable. Roll out to a depth of 1–2mm (just under ⅛ inch) and cut out a 5-petal flower. Press each petal between a veiner to add realistic markings.

Place the petals inside a bun tin or paint palette to firm and set in position (for at least 4 hours).

Place the flower on the foam pad or modelling mat and use the ball tool to frill the petals.

Pinch the tip of each petal to shape.

Use a paintbrush to dust the inside of each petal at the pinch point with a shade of yellow/green colour dust.

MICH'S TIPS

1 When moulding with sugar paste, it is always best to have clean, dry hands. As you knead the sugar paste, it will start to soften and become more pliable and easier to mould and shape.

2 Always work on a small amount of paste at a time as it dries out very quickly.

3 Keep any leftover sugar paste tightly wrapped in cling film in a cool, dry place.

Fill one of the piping bags with white royal icing and pipe a series of white lines, radiating out from the centre of the hellebore.

While the icing is still wet, fix a small pea-sized flattened ball of yellow sugar paste in the centre of the hellebore.

Use a scribe or pokey tool to add more indents over the surface of the yellow centre.

Fill the second piping bag with yellow royal icing and pipe a small yellow pearl (anther) at the outer end of the white strands (filaments) to create the stamens. Leave to dry for 1 hour.

Tutorial Block colour flowers

There are many flower cutters available in various shapes and sizes. I have used one colour to create all the flowers on this cake, and covered the actual tier with the same colour. This creates a striking texture for visual impact. All the flowers can be made in advance and then nudged up to each other on the covered cake. Fix the flowers in position with the same colour royal icing.

Stack the cakes centrally (see pages 154–155). Edge the base and top tier in ivory ribbon and the middle in green. Finish with a bow on the base tier.

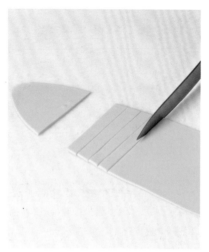

Roll a sheet of petal paste out to a thickness of about 1mm and cut very fine strips about 3mm (⅛ inch) wide.

Wind these strips up to make small, tight spirals.

Leave them for 1 hour or until set and firm. To make the flowers, knead the petal paste until smooth and pliable. Roll out to a thickness of 1–2mm (just under ⅛ inch) and cut out various flowers.

Place the flowers on the foam pad or modelling mat and shape with a ball tool. Leave to shape and set in a paint palette for 1 hour.

Fix the flowers into position with a dab of royal icing piped onto the back of each flower or spiral for precision and less smudging on the cake. Continue until the entire middle tier is covered.

INGREDIENTS

1 x 25cm (10 inch) round cake covered in white sugar paste (see page 145)

1 x 18cm (7 inch) round cake covered in mint green sugar paste (see page 145)

1 x 10cm (4 inch) round cake covered in white sugar paste (see page 145)

250g (9oz) mint green petal paste

Mint green royal icing (see pages 130–133)

YOU WILL ALSO NEED

3m (10ft) of 2.5cm (1 inch) ivory ribbon

1m (40 inches) of 15mm ($^5/_8$ inch) mint green ribbon

Mini rolling pin

Sharp knife

Selection of flower cutters

Foam pad or modelling mat

Ball tool

Piping bag fitted with a No. 2 nozzle

Don't underestimate how many flowers may be required to cover an entire tier – I used 200 on this tier. As they dry they can be stacked. Make sure you have a selection of all shapes.

These delicate frilly flowers are made by rolling the petal paste incredibly thinly, then nicking a small section out from the tip of each petal before they are frilled with the ball tool. This gives the flower a very delicate frilly edge. They are fragile and susceptible to breaking so should be iced directly into place on the cake as soon as they are made to give them maximum support.

INGREDIENTS

Allow 50g (2¾oz) coloured petal paste per flower

Sugar glue

White royal icing (see pages 130–133)

Coloured sugar sprinkles

1 x 5cm (2 inch) crown cake covered in white sugar paste (see page 145) and decorated with rainbow pearls (see page 168)

YOU WILL ALSO NEED

Mini rolling pin

6cm (2½ inch) and 8cm (3¼ inch) 5-petal cutters

Heart cutter

Foam pad or modelling mat

Ball tool

Piping bag fitted with a No. 2 nozzle

Foil cup, to protect

Knead the petal paste until smooth and pliable. Roll out to a depth of about 1mm. Cut out a 5-petal flower in both sizes. Use the tip of a heart cutter to remove an inverse v-section from the tip of each petal. Place the flower on the foam pad or modelling mat and use the ball tool to frill the very edge of the petals.

Fix the 2 flowers together with sugar glue and supported in a foil cup. Fill the piping bag with the white royal icing and pipe a large pearl of icing into the centre of the flower. Sprinkle coloured sugar sprinkles over the icing to stick and leave to dry for about 2 hours until firm and set. Once dry, turn the flower upside down to remove excess sugar sprinkles. Fix the flowers into position on a covered cake with royal icing.

I am often asked how to make a model of a teddy bear that looks cute, realistic and is transportable without the front and back legs falling off. The secret is to create a bear, lying down, with all elements in contact with the cake. This model can be made directly onto the cake. Once mastered the model can be personalized for different celebrations.

TO MAKE THE BEAR

Knead the brown sugar paste until smooth and pliable, then divide in half. Use one half for the body and divide the remaining into 3 portions (head, front legs and ears and back legs). Shape the body into a pear shape, creating a well rounded rump.

Shape the piece for the back legs into a short fat sausage (about 4cm/ 1½ inches big) and slice in half with a sharp knife. Turn the legs so the cut surface is facing down.

Pinch one end together and flatten the pad at the other end to create the shape of the back paw. Repeat with the other leg, shaped the opposite way.

INGREDIENTS

250g (9oz) teddy bear brown sugar paste

20g (¾oz) white sugar paste

20g (¾oz) black sugar paste

YOU WILL ALSO NEED

Sharp knife

Ball tool

Blade tool

Cone tool

Sharp point tool

Smiley tool

Fix into position. Use a ball tool to add the paw detail. Reserve a piece of paste the size of 2 peas from the next portion.

Shape this into a 3cm (1½ inch) sausage. Cut in half, shape and position at the front of the bear's body as shown. Use a blade tool to mark claw details on the front paws.

Shape the piece of paste reserved for the head into a ball, then draw the snout forward to a point and shape the back of the head up ready for the ears. Place in position resting on the front legs, at a jaunty angle.

Roll the 2 pea-shaped balls of paste for the ears and flatten slightly. Hold the ear in position on the bear's head and fix into position by inserting the cone tool into the ear and head together. Repeat with the other ear.

Insert the sharp point tool into the bear's head to make the eye sockets.

Roll a small cone of white sugar paste and insert this into the eye socket. Repeat for the other eye.

Roll a small ball of black paste and flatten slightly into position on to each of the bear's eyes to add the pupils. Shape a small ball of black paste into a triangle and fix this in position for the bear's nose (dampen with a little water to help fix).

Finally, use the smiley tool to indent a smile at a jaunty angle to give the bear personality.

FOR THE HENRI BEAR

So sweet to give the teddy bears real character. This simple addition of a black sugar paste beret and a hand-painted moustache using black colour gel and a fine paintbrush turns the teddy bear into our suave and rather dashing Henri! Bonjour Monsieur!

BRIDAL BEAR CAKE

This design is lovely for a hen party or bridal shower to celebrate the impending nuptials of the blushing bride. This design can also work well for a Holy Communion, Confirmation celebration or Princess birthday. The veil has been textured and lustred before being cut out, adding more detail and texture.

INGREDIENTS

1 x 15cm (6 inch) round cake covered in white sugar paste (page 145)

150g (5½ oz) white sugar paste

Edible pearl lustre

1 x Hand-moulded Teddy Bear (see pages 218–219)

3 tablespoons white royal icing

1 teaspoon light green royal icing

YOU WILL ALSO NEED

1m (40 inches) of 2.5cm (1 inch) pretty ribbon

1m (40 inches) of 3cm (1¼ inch) grosgrain ribbon

Cake stand

Mini rolling pin

Impression rolling pin

Sharp knife

Piping bag fitted with a No. 106 nozzle

Waxed paper or Bake-O-Glide

Edge the cake in pretty ribbon and place on a decorative cake stand.

Knead the white sugar paste until smooth and pliable, then roll out to a thickness of 3mm (⅛ inch). Roll an impression pin over the surface of the paste to create the pattern. Spray the surface of the rolled paste with pearl lustre, then leave to dry for a few seconds.

Cut out a pear shape of paste with a sharp knife, it should be about the size of the teddy bear's body and head.

Lift the veil into position, fixing it firmly between the bear's ears and allowing it to trail outwards over the bear's body.

Fill the piping bag with the No. 106 nozzle and white royal icing and pipe flowers onto a sheet of waxed paper or Bake-O-Glide, then leave to dry overnight.

Peel the flowers off the waxed paper or Bake-O-Glide and fix into position for the bear's head and bouquet. Add more piped flowers as detail around the cake and add small hand-piped green leaves to the bouquet to finish.

"Use an impression pin and spray lustre to add detail to the bridal veil."

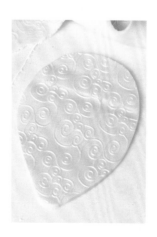

Tutorial Cutting shapes

There is a real charm in creating cakes with a nostalgic design as they can never date! This vintage perambulator cake is given a gentle, modern influence by using a muted palette suitable for girls and boys. The technique is a simple découpage with hand-piped detail. Prepare the templates and cut out all the shapes before you start to fix them on the cake.

Edge the cake in the cream ribbon and the board in the blue ribbon. Working with a small piece of each colour at a time, roll out the petal paste to a depth of 1–2mm (just under ⅛ inch) and cut out an 8cm (3 ½ inch) circle.

Cut the circle in half to make 2 bases for the perambulators.

Cut out two 3cm (1¼ inch) diameter circles for the wheels.

Use the template on page 259 to cut out 3 panels for the hood.

Moisten the back of the pram base with water or sugar glue and fix into position on the side of the cake.

Moisten the back of the wheels and fix these into position.

INGREDIENTS

1 x 25cm (10 inch) round cake covered in buttermilk-coloured sugar paste (see page 145)

50g (2¾oz) petal paste in each colour (blue, buttermilk, pistachio and creamy yellow)

1 tablespoon buttermilk-coloured royal icing (see pages 130–133)

YOU WILL ALSO NEED

1m (40 inches) of 2.5cm (1 inch) cream grosgrain ribbon for the cake

35cm (14 inch) square drum board lined with yellow sugar paste

1.75m (5¾ft) of 15mm (⅝ inch) blue ribbon for the base board

8cm (3½ inch) and 3cm (1½ inch) round cutters

Perambulator template (see page 259)

Sharp knife

Piping bag fitted with a No. 1.5 nozzle

MICH'S TIPS

1 Petal paste will dry out quickly. Keep the cut out shapes under a sheet of plastic and use different colours to make up each perambulator.

2 Upturn a 20cm (8 inch) cake board on the top of the cake and score around with a scribe or pokey tool – use this as a template to hand pipe a ring of pearls.

3 Fix a découpage perambulator on the top of the cake or use this space to hand pipe a message or name for a Christening cake.

4 For this 25cm (10 inch) cake I made a total of 10 perambulators.

5 Use this same template to make cookies that can be decorated to match.

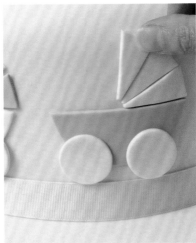

Fix the 3 panels for the hood into position. Fill the piping bag with buttermilk-coloured royal icing.

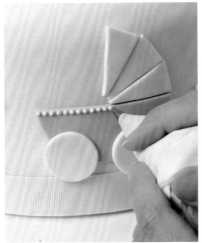

Pipe pearls across the pram; repeat around the cake. Make a pram for the top. Pipe pearls around the top of the cake.

FONDANT FANCIES

These cakes have been covered in marzipan and fondant and hand-decorated with cut-out shapes. The icing is very sweet so choose a well flavoured, moist cake. Almond, lemon, vanilla or orange whisked cakes work well. These cakes have been fully enrobed and left to set, but they can be placed in foil cases and the edges pressed as it can be difficult to achieve a neat edge with fondant. Fondant is relatively inexpensive, takes colours well and is an easier way to cover smaller, more intricately shaped fun party cakes.

Makes 4 fondant fancies

INGREDIENTS

4 x 6cm (2½ inch) diameter round cakes cut out of a 23cm (9 inch) baked whisked cake (see pages 50–51)

Alllow 2 teaspoons apricot jam per cake

Alllow 50–75g (1¾–2¾oz) marzipan per cake

Allow 500g (1lb 2oz) fondant icing sugar for 6–8 cakes (depending on the depth of cake)

5g (⅛oz) sugar paste and colours per shape

Coloured edible glitter

YOU WILL ALSO NEED

6cm (2½ inch) round cutters

Non-stick baking parchment

Disposable piping bags

Shape cutters for decoration

Paintbrush

Sugar glue

Stamp out rounds of cake using a 6cm (2½ inch) round cutter.

Put the apricot jam in a saucepan and heat gently until melted. Use a pastry brush to brush the surface of the cakes with melted jam.

Use the same cutter to stamp out discs of marzipan and place one on top of each round cake.

Place the cakes on a wire cooling rack with space between each and a sheet of non-stick baking parchment underneath the rack to contain excess fondant.

Make the fondant according to the packet instructions. Fill a large disposable piping bag with freshly made fondant and snip the end with sharp scissors.

Pipe the fondant over the top and sides of the cakes and tap the wire rack to settle and level the icing (see pages 150–151).

Leave to settle for a few minutes, then remove the cakes with a small crank-handled palette knife. Trim the edges and place the cakes on a pretty plate or into a foil case.

Cut out coloured shapes of sugar paste, brush with sugar glue and sprinkle with coloured edible glitter. Position a shape carefully on the top of each fondant cake.

CHRISTMAS CROWN CAKES

Undoubtedly, one of the highlights in our calendar is my annual Indulgent Christmas Masterclass. We hold this at one of London's most esteemed hotels and students enjoy a day decorating crown cakes, cookies and Christmas cakes, before celebrating with a Champagne Afternoon Tea. My challenge is to design new Christmas crown cakes every year. These are some of my favourites.

HAND-PIPED STAR

Roll the white sugar paste to a thickness of 2mm (just under ⅛ inch) and cut out a star large enough to sit on top of the cake.

Moisten the back of the star with a little water and place in position on the top of the cake.

INGREDIENTS

1 x 5cm (2 inch) crown cake, covered in marzipan and white sugar paste and edged in 15mm (⅝ inch) white grosgrain ribbon (see pages 140–149)

75g (2¾oz) white sugar paste

1 tablespoon white royal icing (see pages 130–133)

YOU WILL ALSO NEED

Rolling pin

5cm (2 inch) star cutter

Piping bag fitted with a No. 1.5 nozzle

Fill the piping bag with white royal icing and pipe a series of rows of pearls at the tip of each arm of the star starting with 1 pearl and finishing with 5 pearls.

Hold the piping bag with the tip vertically over the centre and pipe a loop to the base of each star point.

Pipe a pearl between each loop and finish with a larger pearl in the centre of the cake.

POINSETTIA

INGREDIENTS

Red petal paste

Edible spray glue

Red shimmer dust

1 x 5cm (2 inch) crown cake, covered in marzipan and white sugar paste and edged in 15mm (⁵⁄₈ inch) red grosgrain ribbon (see pages 140–149)

1 tablespoon stiff green royal icing

1 teaspoon yellow royal icing

YOU WILL ALSO NEED

Rolling pin

5cm (2 inch) calyx cutter

Foam pad or modelling mat

Ball toll

Piping bag fitted with a No. 69 leaf nozzle

Piping bag fitted with a No. 1.5 nozzle

Roll the red petal paste to 1mm (under ⅛ inch) thick. Use a 5cm (2 inch) calyx cutter to cut out 2 flowers per poinsettia.

Place the calyx on a foam pad or modelling mat and use a ball tool to shape and curl the petals.

Spray each flower separately with edible spray glue and dust with red shimmer dust. Leave to set for 1 hour.

Fix the 2 flowers together held in place with sugar glue and leave to set for 1 hour.

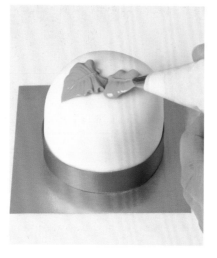

Fill the piping bag fitted with the leaf nozzle with stiff green royal icing and pipe 3 leaves on the top of the crown cake (see page 114).

Lift the poinsettia into place and press down into the leaves. Fill the other piping bag with yellow icing and pipe pearls in the centre of the poinsettia.

FAIRY LIGHTS

INGREDIENTS

1 x 5cm (2 inch) crown cake, covered in marzipan and white sugar paste and edged in 15mm (⁵⁄₈ inch) red grosgrain ribbon (see pages 140–149)

1 teaspoon each of green, yellow, red and blue royal icing

YOU WILL ALSO NEED

Piping bag fitted with a No. 1.2 nozzle

3 piping bags fitted with No. 2 nozzles

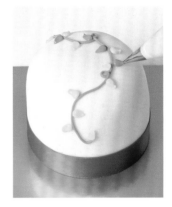

Fill the piping bag fitted with the No. 1.5 nozzle with green royal icing and pipe a swirly trail over the top and side of the cake (the light wire).

Fit one of the remaining piping bags with yellow icing and pipe a series of pearl drops coming from the green strand to represent the yellow lights.

Fill another piping bag with red royal icing and pipe the red lights into position. Repeat with blue to finish.

CHRISTMAS PUDDING

INGREDIENTS

25g (1oz) white sugar paste

1 x 5cm (2 inch) crown cake, covered in marzipan and brown sugar paste and edged in 15mm (¾ inch) brown grosgrain ribbon (see pages 140–149)

Green petal paste, for the leaves

1 teaspoon royal icing

Red petal or sugar paste, for the berries

Red shimmer dust

YOU WILL ALSO NEED

Rolling pin

Holly plunger cutter

Star cutter

Roll out white sugar paste to a depth of 2mm (just under ⅛ inch) and cut out a star large enough to sit on top of the cake. Moisten the back with a little water and place in position on the cake. Mould the edges of the star into the cake.

Roll the green petal paste to 1–2mm (just under ⅛ inch) thick and use the holly plunger cutter to cut and vein holly leaves. Fix into position with royal icing.

Roll balls of red petal paste and drop into a dish of red shimmer dust. Leave to set for

1 hour, then fix in the middle of the leaves, holding in position with a little royal icing.

MICH'S TIPS

1 Try different shades of green or adding lustre or shimmer dust to the holly for added detail.

2 Box these little cakes for the perfect Christmas present for teachers, family and friends. They can be made from different flavours to add contrast and variety.

HOBBY HORSE COOKIES

Makes 10–12 cookies

INGREDIENTS

200g (7oz) unsalted butter

200g (7oz) golden caster sugar

1 medium egg, beaten

400g (14oz) plain flour, plus extra for dusting

2 teaspoons vanilla bean paste

TO DECORATE (PER COOKIE)

50g (1¾oz) pale green sugar paste (see page 144)

1 tablespoon each of red, brown and black royal icing (see pages 130–133)

YOU WILL ALSO NEED

Rolling pin

Hobby horse template (see page 261)

20cm (8 inch) lolly sticks

1 piping bag fitted with No. 2 nozzle

2 piping bags fitted with No. 1.5 nozzles

10–12 x 3mm (⅛ inch) red ribbon bows

Preheat the oven to 180°C (350°F/Gas 4).

These extra thick vanilla cookies have been baked onto lolly sticks and then decorated, making them perfect for party favours. These cookies can be wrapped in cellophane or decorated plastic cookie bags and labelled with the name of each guest.

Cream the butter and sugar together, then add the beaten egg to combine. Gently fold in the flour and vanilla bean paste and mix until a dough combines. Wrap the dough in cling film and chill for 30 minutes.

Lightly flour a work surface and roll the dough out to a thickness of 1cm (½ inch). Use the template on page 261 to cut out the hobby horses. Insert 4–5cm (1½–2 inch) of a lolly stick in the base of each horse's head. Lift the shapes onto a non-stick baking sheet and bake for 20 minutes until golden and crisp. Leave to cool for a few minutes before transferring to a wire rack to cool completely.

Roll the green sugar paste out to 1–2mm (just under ⅛ inch) thick and cut out horse's head shapes. Fix in position with a little royal icing. Fill the piping bag fitted with the No. 2 nozzle with red royal icing and pipe strands of hair for the mane. Start close to the head and pipe outwards. Fix a red ribbon bow at the base of each head using royal icing.

Fill the piping bags fitted with the No 1.5 nozzles with brown royal icing and black royal icing and pipe the bridle and a single black eye. Leave to set and dry.

Storage: These cookies can be made and decorated in advance. They will keep for 7 days if kept in an airtight container.

"Don't roll the cookie dough too thin as the lolly stick will not hold and the cookie might break."

BRIDE & GROOM WEDDING

We have affectionately named our happy couple Margaret and Steve. These charming bride and groom cookies make wonderful wedding favours or place settings at a wedding. They can be made up to 10 days in advance and wrapped in cellophane bags tied with pretty ribbon.

Makes 8–10 cookies

INGREDIENTS

1 quantity Vanilla Cookie dough (see page 231)

Allow 50g (1¾oz) each of white, black, brown and natural sugar paste per couple (see page 144)

Pearl lustre

Allow 1 teaspoon each of black, white and natural royal icing per couple (see pages 130–133)

Colour dusts (optional)

YOU WILL ALSO NEED

Mini rolling pin

Bride & groom templates (see page 260)

Sharp knife

Impression rolling pin

Small or 5mm (¼ inch) blossom plunger cutter

Disposable piping bags

Preheat the oven 180°C (350°F/Gas 4).

Make the cookie dough as described on page 231. Roll out to 5mm (¼ inch) thick and use the templates to cut out the bride and groom shapes. Transfer to a non-stick baking sheet and bake for 10 minutes until light golden. Leave to cool for a few seconds, then transfer to a wire rack until completely cool.

Roll the natural sugar paste out to a thickness of 2mm (just under ⅛ inch) and use the templates to cut out the heads and bride's arms. Fix in position with royal icing.

Roll the white sugar paste out to 2mm (just under ⅛ inch) thick and use the templates to cut out the groom's shirt and the bride's dress (use an impression pin over the icing to add detail to the dress before cutting out, which

can then be sprayed with pearl lustre). Fix in position with a little royal icing. Stamp out 5 plunger blossoms.

Roll the black sugar paste out to a thickness of 2mm (just under ⅛ inch) and cut out the groom's hat and suit and the bride's hair. Fix in position with royal icing.

Roll and cut the groom's hair from brown sugar paste. Shape 2 small rounded pearls of black paste for the bow tie. Hand-pipe black eyes and neutral mouths. Add desired coloured dust to the blossoms and fix in position to represent the bouquet, button hole and flower in the bride's hair. Hand pipe a handkerchief for the groom. Leave to set, then wrap individually in clear cellophane bags.

CHRISTMAS COOKIES

I love creating cookies that can be decorated, threaded with a ribbon and hung on the Christmas tree. They add a real point of difference and individuality each year and are a fun project to undertake with the children.

Makes about 12 cookies

INGREDIENTS

250g (9oz) plain flour

1 teaspoon ground cinnamon

½ teaspoon ground nutmeg

½ teaspoon ground ginger

125g (4½oz) unsalted butter

125g (4½oz) light brown sugar

50g (1¾oz) ground almonds

½ teaspoon almond extract

1 large egg, beaten

YOU WILL ALSO NEED

Rolling pin

Templates (see pages 259–260)

7.5cm (3 inch) round cutter

3.5cm (1½ inch) fluted cutter

Straw or skewer

Preheat the oven to 180°C (350°F/Gas 4).

Sift the flour and spices into a bowl. Rub the butter into the flour until it resembles fine breadcrumbs. Stir in the sugar, almonds and almond extract. Stir in the beaten egg to bind the dough and knead into a ball. Wrap the dough in cling film and chill for 30 minutes. Roll out the dough to 5–7mm (¼–¾ inch) thick. To make the wreath cookies, cut out plain rounds, then cut an inner circle out using a fluted cutter. Use the templates to cut skate and crown cookies. Transfer the shapes to a non-stick baking sheet with a palette knife. Insert the end of a straw or skewer to make the hole for threading the ribbon. Bake for 10–12 minutes until baked and golden. Leave to cool for a few seconds, then lift onto a wire rack to cool completely.

TO DECORATE A WREATH COOKIE

INGREDIENTS

2 tablespoons stiff green royal icing (see pages 130–133) per cookie

Red and gold berries – 3 each per cookie

YOU WILL ALSO NEED

Piping bag

Ribbon bow

Tweezers

30cm (12 inches) of 3mm (⅛ inch) wide ribbon, to thread

Fill the piping bag with the green icing. Snip across the top of the bag at an angle, then back the opposite way to create an open v-shape on the top. Using two hands, pressure pipe a green garland around the wreath. Start at the top and come down each side to the base.

While the icing is still wet, fix the ribbon bow in position and use a pair of tweezers to place the gold and red berries in place. Leave to dry, then thread a length of ribbon through the hole and tie a knot.

TO DECORATE A SKATE COOKIE

INGREDIENTS (PER COOKIE)

50g (1¾oz) each of red and chocolate sugar paste (see page 144)

1 tablespoon white royal icing (see pages 130–133)

YOU WILL ALSO NEED

Mini rolling pin

Sharp knife

Star modelling tool

Piping bag fitted with No. 2 nozzle

Piping bag fitted with No. 5 star nozzle

Ribbon, to thread

MICH'S TIPS

1 Change the colours of the skate and crowns to complement your Christmas theme colours.

2 Wrap a single cookie in cellophane and use it as a present tag – with a hand-piped name on each cookie.

3 These cookies will be edible for 7 days, but can be left on the Christmas tree for up to 14 days as a decoration.

4 Omit the ribbon holes before baking and present a selection of decorated cookies ina pretty box lined with tissue as the perfect festive gift.

Roll the red sugar paste to a thickness of 2mm (just under ⅛ inch) and cut out the skate using the template on page 260.

Fix this into position on the cookie using a little royal icing to hold it in place. Mark a pattern on top using the star tool.

Fill the piping bag fitted with the No. 2 nozzle with white royal icing and pipe the base of the skate underneath the red sugar paste, enhancing the toe and heel.

Roll a sausage of chocolate sugar paste and taper one end to a point. Curl this upwards and press into position at the base of the skate cookie. Trim the end to sharpen and neaten.

Fill the piping bag fitted with the No. 5 star nozzle with white royal icing and pipe a zigzag of icing at the top of the skate, being careful not to cover the hole. Leave to dry, then thread a length of ribbon through the hole and tie a knot.

TO DECORATE A CROWN COOKIE

Fill a piping bag with natural royal icing and pipe the outline of the crown, 3mm (⅛ inch) inside the edge of the cookie. Pipe a circle around the hole.

Thin the icing down to a flooding consistency and flood the inside of the cookie (see page 133).

Use a paintbrush to draw the icing to the corners of the crown. Leave to skin over for 30–60 minutes.

Fill a piping bag with white royal icing and pipe the detail at the base of the crown with a series of lines and pearls.

Pipe 3 fleur de lys emblems on the crown and join these with scallops.

Finish by piping a series of pearls around the outline of the crown. Leave to dry, then thread a length of ribbon through the hole and tie a knot.

INGREDIENTS (PER COOKIE)

2 tablespoons each of natural (or gold) and white royal icing (see pages 130–133)

YOU WILL ALSO NEED

2 piping bags fitted with No. 2 nozzles

Paintbrush

Ribbon, to thread

"Alternate the colours of flooding and piping icing to create a contrast of designs."

Hand Painting

Hand painting on cakes combines two of my passions – the design options are endless. I find the whole painting process therapeutic and always underestimate the length of time it takes to hand paint a cake. Painting is less daunting than piping and can be an effective decoration for beginners. My technique involves melting cocoa butter and blending with colour dusts to build up painted layers. It is worth highlighting that to create a translucent water colour effect, use more cocoa butter and less colour dust. For a more solid block painting, akin to an oil painting, add more colour dust compound and blend colours with white colour dust for an opaque effect. Keep a board lined with sugar paste next to your celebration cake to act as a sample palette to check colour intensities and shades. Use absorbent kitchen paper to clean the paintbrushes between strokes or when changing colours.

Lucky ladybirds are simple and effective. I have chosen to cover this crown cake with the red painted bugs with delicate authentic attention to detail. Practise on some board to build up your confidence when trying out a new design.

INGREDIENTS

1 x 5cm (2 inch) crown cake, covered in marzipan and white sugar paste and edged in 15mm (¾ inch) orange ribbon (see pages 140–149)

5g (1 teaspoon) cocoa butter

¼ teaspoon each of red, black, and ivory colour dusts

YOU WILL ALSO NEED

Selection of paintbrushes

Ladybird template (see page 259) or paint free hand

Begin by painting the red bodies of the ladybirds. Blend cocoa butter with red colour dust and paint at intervals over the cake – these should be elongated circles with a point at one end and a flat top at the head. Use the template on page 259 as a guide.

With a superfine paintbrush, add the black detail at the head of the ladybird and across the top of the body. Paint a curled line down through the body. Add the spots to the body – an equal number and position on each side.

Paint the ivory detail on the head of the ladybird. Finish by hand painting the legs.

MICH'S TIP

Allow each section to dry before painting the detail on top. Work by painting the same element of each ladybird in sequence so by the time all the bodies have been painted the first will have dried sufficiently to begin the next stage.

This technique combines two techniques: hand painting the base of the lotus flowers from the top down over the side of the crown cake and hand piping the outline in a contrasting colour. Finish with hand-piped perfect pearls.

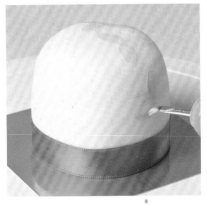

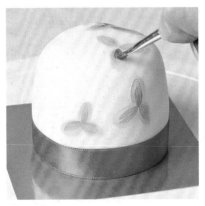

INGREDIENTS

1 x 5cm (2 inch) crown cake, covered in marzipan and white sugar paste and edged in 15mm (¾ inch) orange ribbon (see pages 140–149)

5g (1 teaspoon) cocoa butter

¼ teaspoon each of orange and yellow colour dusts

2 teaspoons orange royal icing (see pages 130–133)

YOU WILL ALSO NEED

Lotus flower template (see page 261) or paint free hand

Selection of paintbrushes

Piping bag fitted with a No. 1.5 nozzle

Begin by painting the 3 pronged lotus flower in a base colour on the cake using the lotus flower template as a guide. Add a second darker colour down through the centre of the first colour before the base coat has time to set. Paint a third colour just in the centre of the lotus flower.

Fill the piping bag with orange icing and pipe the outline of the lotus flower petals and add a stalk. Fill in the gaps with clusters of delicate piped pearls.

Change the colour of these lotus flowers and ribbon to complement your celebration.

ART NOUVEAU BUTTERFLY

This striking design cleverly combines a cut-out butterfly with hand painting and hand piping. The technique is simple and the effect impressive. Change the colour and size of the butterflies to create variations. This technique translates well to birthday, anniversary, celebration and wedding cakes. All the detail is applied once the butterfly is in situ on the cake, minimizing any possible damage.

INGREDIENTS

1 x 20cm (8 inch) round cake covered in white sugar paste (see page 145)

1 x 10cm (4 inch) round cake covered in white sugar paste (see page 145)

50g (1¾oz) orange sugar paste (see page 144)

1 teaspoon black colour dust

1–2 teaspoons alcohol rejuvenator spirit

2 tablespoons white royal icing (see pages 130–133)

5 x Hand-moulded Hellebore Roses (see pages 212–213), to finish

YOU WILL ALSO NEED

2.5cm (1 inch) orange double satin ribbon

Cake stand

Mini rolling pin

Butterfly template (see page 259)

Sharp knife

Paintbrush

Piping bag fitted with a No. 1.5 nozzle

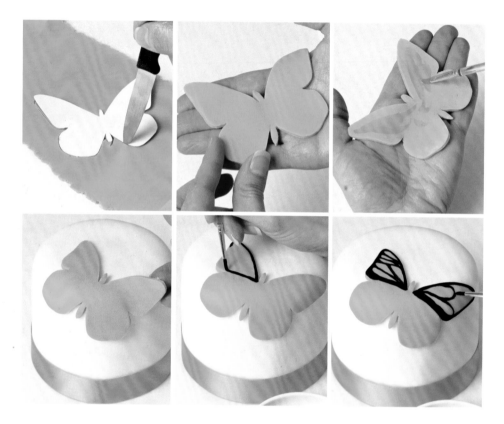

Stack the cakes centrally following the instructions on pages 154–155 and edge the base of each tier with the orange ribbon. Place the cake on a decorative cake stand.

Knead the orange sugar paste until smooth and pliable. Roll out to a thickness of 3mm (⅛ inch). Place the butterfly template on the surface and use a sharp knife to carefully cut around it. Neaten and smooth the edges of the butterfly carefully with your fingers. Flip the butterfly over and dampen the back with a little cooled boiled water.

Lay the butterfly directly onto the top tier, moulding it over the edge of the cake and rubbing and pressing it into position.

Blend the black colour dust with the rejuvenator spirit in a little bowl and paint the details on the top wings as shown.

Add the veining detail to the top wings, making sure they are symmetrical. Paint the detail on the lower wings and paint the central body of the butterfly.

Fill the piping bag with white royal icing and pipe a trail of random white pearls around the outside edge of the butterfly. Continue piping the pearls until the outside edge of the butterfly is fully decorated, then leave to dry. Repeat this process on a second butterfly on the base tier. Dress the cake with hand-moulded hellebores to finish.

Ribbon loops are an effective way to add colour and vibrancy to projects. Double satin, organza or grosgrain ribbon can be used to make wired loops. The optimum ribbon thicknesses are 9mm (³/8 inch), 12mm (¹/2 inch) and 15mm (⁵/8 inch) wide – it is more fiddly to work with thinner or thicker.

YOU WILL NEED

35cm (14 inches) ribbon for each loop

26-gauge wire

Floristry tape

MICH'S TIPS

1 Double satin ribbon is the perfect ribbon to create ribbon loops.

2 Both grosgrain and organza ribbons can be used but their thickness and sheen respectively make them a little trickier to tape up.

3 I have shown triple loops with a tail but you can make a selection of single loops and double loops depending on your preference.

You must put a fold in the ribbon to turn the tail back so it is pointing in the same direction as the loops, before wiring and taping.

With the cut end of ribbon facing away from you, make a loop and hold this between your first and second finger. This loop should be able to stand up and not flop over.

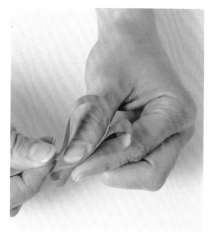

Fold the length of ribbon over to make a second loop the same height as the first, lining up at the base.

Repeat to make a third loop and then fold the ribbon back as though to make a fourth loop, but cut it straight – and leave this as a tail about 10cm (4 inches) long.

Turn the loop and tail over and hold between your thumb and finger. Take a 15cm (6 inch) length of 26-gauge wire behind the base of the loop and position it with one long end of wire and one short end of wire either side of the ribbon.

Fold the base of the ribbon loop over this wire. Hold in position with your third finger and fold the shorter end of wire back.

Fold the longer end of wire back so the wires cross in the centre.

Twist the two lengths of wire together tightly to seal the ribbon loop.

Thread a length of floristry tape behind the wire of the ribbon loop to hide it and fold the short end back over. Give the floristry tape a gentle tug as you pull it to activate the self-seal stickiness.

Continue to wrap the floristry tape around and down the length of the wire to seal, neaten and strengthen. Pull the tape against the wire to cut the tape.

TOUCAN TANGO

INGREDIENTS

1 x 25cm (10 inch) round cake covered in coloured sugar paste (see pages 145)

1 x 15cm (6 inch) round cake covered in coloured sugar paste (see page 145)

3 x Hand-moulded Gloriosa Lilies (see pages 206–207)

3 x Hand-moulded Lemons (see below)

3 x Hand-moulded Limes (see below)

Selection of colour dusts (black, yellow, green, blue, white, crimson)

2 teaspoons cocoa butter

1 tablespoon royal icing (see pages 130–133)

YOU WILL ALSO NEED

Different colour 2.5cm (1 inch) thick ribbons for edging the cakes

1 x 35cm (14 inch) round cake board lined with sugar paste

15mm (⅝ inch) fuchsia ribbon

Scribe/pokey tool

18 Ribbon Loops (see page 244–245) in a selection of colours, widths and finishes

Selection of paintbrushes

Toucan templates (see page 260)

Floristry tape

3 fat posy picks

Disposable piping bag

Wooden cocktail sticks

I love the vibrancy of this cake with all its elements of Rio and mardi gras carnival. An explosion of colour and showcasing several techniques – hand painting, gloriosa lilies, ribbon loops and hand-moulded lemons and limes. Colour the sugar paste to reflect the flavours of the cakes inside. I feel a salsa coming on!

 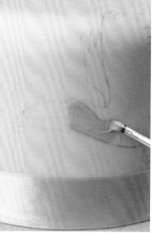 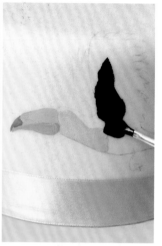

Stack the cakes centrally (see pages 154–155) and edge the base of each tier with double ribbons. Edge the cake board with fuchsia ribbon and place the stacked cake on the board.

Trace the toucan and hummingbirds using a scribe or pokey tool onto the cake at strategic positions. Begin by painting the base colours of each of the birds, allowing the sections to dry before adding more layers. Add more layers of paint, using the brushstrokes to highlight the birds' feathers, then leave to dry.

To assemble, tape 6 ribbon loops to the base of each gloriosa lily to create a corsage. Insert the posy picks into the cake and fill with royal icing. Trim the wires at the base of the corsage and insert into the posy pick. The royal icing will help the corsage to set firm.

Half thread the lemons and limes (see below) onto cocktail sticks and push the remaining halves into the cake to hold the fruit in position.

TO MAKE THE LEMONS & LIMES

Knead a large walnut-sized piece of yellow or green sugar paste until smooth and pliable. Shape into a lemon or lime shape – round with slightly tapered ends. Press a wire wool sponge over the surface to create a dimpled peel effect. Insert a star tool at one end to create the top, then leave to firm up overnight. Dust the fruit with a blend of yellow or green colour dusts to highlight the different shades of the peel.

Hand-painted handmade sugar butterflies never fail to impress when added to delicate christening or birthday cakes. They also create a fantastic statement as I have shown here with this stunning wedding cake. They are time-consuming to make, but as easy to make three dozen as it is to make a handful. Once the wings are iced, dried and painted the butterflies can be stored flat for up to 3 months and the bodies hand piped and butterflies created as needed.

INGREDIENTS

1 x 25cm (10 inch) round cake covered in marzipan and white sugar paste (see pages 140–145)

1 x 18cm (7 inch) round cake (cut from a 20cm/8 inch cake) covered in marzipan and white sugar paste

1 x 10cm (4 inch) round cake covered in marzipan and white sugar paste

FOR THE BUTTERFLIES (MAKES 30)

4 tablespoons white royal icing (see pages 130–133)

10 tablespoons orange flooding icing (see page 133)

1 teaspoon each black, yellow and white colour dust

1 teaspoon cocoa butter

4 tablespoons black royal icing (see pages 130–133)

YOU WILL ALSO NEED

32.5cm (13 inch) round lined double depth cake board

3m (10ft) of 25mm (1 inch) black double satin ribbon

3m (10ft) of 15mm (⅝ inch) orange grosgrain ribbon

2 piping bags fitted with No.2 nozzles; and 1 with No.3 nozzle

Template (see page 258)

Non-stick baking parchment

Disposable piping bags or squeezie bottle

Paintbrush

Stack the cakes centrally (see pages 154–155). Edge the base of each tier and the board with both ribbons. Fill a piping bag fitted with a No.2 nozzle with white icing. Pipe pearls above the ribbon on all 3 tiers, random and various sizes.

Trace the template of the butterfly onto paper and fix on a work board with masking tape. Place non-stick baking parchment over the template and fix with masking tape. Fill a piping bag fitted with a No. 2 nozzle with white royal icing. Pipe the outline of the butterfly.

Fill a piping bag or squeezie bottle with thinner orange flooding icing. Hold the tip of the bag or squeezie bottle in the icing so as not to incorporate air bubbles and fill the top wings with icing. Use a paintbrush held vertically and, making small circular movements, draw the icing into all the corners. Use the paintbrush to burst any tiny air bubbles that may rise to the surface. Leave to dry for 30 minutes

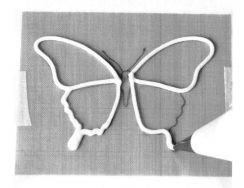
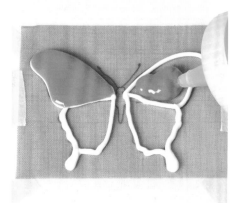
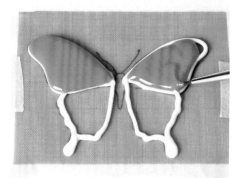

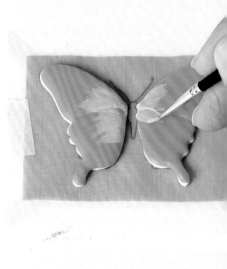

Flood the base wings with the same colour royal icing making sure not to push the icing into the top wings. Leave to dry overnight.

Melt a little cocoa butter and mix with yellow colour dust. Paint the centre of the butterfly wings, fanning outwards to create a feather-like texture. Paint the tips and base of the wings with black colour dust mixed with melted cocoa butter, making sure to cover right down to the paper. Allow to dry for about 2 hours.

Stipple the wings with shots of white colour dust mixed with melted cocoa butter to create the detail on the butterfly. Leave to dry overnight.

Carefully insert a small cranked handle palette knife under each wing to remove from the baking parchment.

Always make extra butterflies than you need to replace any casualties if you are transporting the cake to a venue. Transport the butterflies separately and fix them on once the cake is in situ.

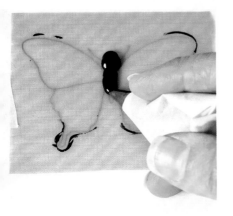
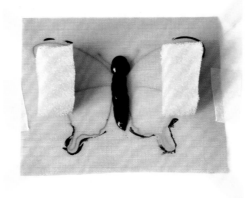

Fill a piping bag with No. 3 nozzle and stiff black royal icing. Pipe a head and long body in the centre of the butterfly template.

Position two small 1cm (½ inch) squares of sponge either side of the butterfly's central body. Fix the wings carefully into position either side of the central body with the wings resting on the sponge squares to support until dry – leave overnight.

When you are ready to fix the butterfly on the cake, remove the sponge from beneath the wings and use a cranked handle palette knife to remove the butterfly from the paper.

Carefully hold one of the wings and flip it over. Pipe a small trail of white royal icing along the body of the butterfly and carefully fix into position on the cake. Hold for a few moments for the icing to firm.

EASTER COOKIES

I wanted to include Easter biscuits – with a more grown up feel. These delicate egg-shaped lemon and almond biscuits have been decorated with fresh pastel colours and hand-piped with delicate white detail.

Makes about 16 cookies

INGREDIENTS

150g (5½oz) unsalted butter

150g (5½oz) golden caster sugar

300g (10½oz) plain flour

Grated zest of 2 lemons

55g (2oz) ground almonds

1 teaspoon almond extract

1 medium egg, beaten

Royal icing in fresh spring shades and white (see pages 130–133) – allow 2 tablespoons per cookie

YOU WILL ALSO NEED

Easter egg template (see page 259)

2 piping bags fitted with No. 1.5 nozzles

Paintbrush

Extra piping bags or a squeezie bottle

Preheat the oven to 180°C (350°F/ Gas 4).

"I love to make batches of these cookies and use them for an Easter egg hunt instead of chocolate eggs."

Cream the butter and sugar together, then gently fold in the flour, lemon zest, almonds and almond extract and enough egg to form a stiff dough. Wrap in cling film and chill for 30 minutes. Roll out the dough to a thickness of 5mm (¼ inch) and use the templates to cut out the egg shapes. Transfer to a non-stick baking sheet and bake for 10-12 minutes until baked and golden. Leave to cool for a few seconds, then lift onto a wire rack to cool completely.

Fill a piping bag fitted with the No. 1.5 nozzle with coloured royal icing. Pipe the outline of the egg 3mm (⅛ inch) inside the edge of the biscuit.

Thin the icing down to a flooding consistency (see page 133) and flood the inside of the biscuit.

Use a paintbrush to draw the icing to the corners of the egg, then leave to skin over for 30–60 minutes.

Fill the second piping bag with white royal icing and pipe the bow detail at the top of the egg and flood with white royal icing.

Use a paintbrush to draw the icing to the edges of the bow.

Pipe a series of stems at the base of the biscuit to resemble stalks.

Add hand piped flower details to the cookie, then leave to set.

Storage: These will keep for 7 days.

Tutorial Applying gold leaf

Edible gold leaf has traditionally been used to add a touch of refined opulence to patisserie and desserts. Impressive, perfectly safe to eat, yet expensive and difficult to handle, I want to show you how to work with gold leaf to apply it to an entire cake tier for impact and real wow factor. Edible gold leaf comes in books of 10 or more 10cm (4 inch) square sheets. Gold leaf is susceptible to touch and moisture. The easiest way to handle it – is not to handle it!

Apply gold leaf the day before to ensure the cake is firm and set. Place on a sheet of non-stick baking parchment and spray with clear edible gel glue. The cake should be tacky, but not wet.

Open up one page to expose a square of gold leaf and hold the book at the spine for support.

Press the book against the cake to allow the gold leaf to transfer from the book to the tacky glue on the cake.

Ease the gold leaf into position using the non-stick paper in the book.

Edible gold leaf can be used to cover large surfaces, such as an entire cake tier, or used to decorate smaller pieces such as chocolates, sugar flowers or fresh fruit (see below).

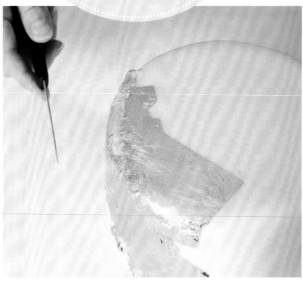

Repeat with more sheets until the entire tier is covered. Be careful to overlap the edges of the gold leaf, to avoid seams, and make sure there are no bare patches.

Use the tip of a knife to gently tease any final remaining pieces of gold leaf into place, then finish with another spray of edible gel glue all over the cake to fix into position. Leave to dry.

Use a paintbrush to dampen the surface of fresh cherries with water, then press gold leaf onto the cherries with a clean paintbrush.

GILDED CHRISTMAS CAKE

The crowning glory for any festive Christmas table. This cake celebrates many of the techniques learnt in this book. Be inspired to mix and match your favoured designs and techniques to create your own special centrepiece.

INGREDIENTS

1 x 10cm (4 inch) round cake covered in marzipan and white sugar paste (see pages 140–145)

1 x 15cm (6 inch) round cake covered in marzipan and white sugar paste (see pages 140–145)

1 x 20cm (8 inch) round cake covered in marzipan and white sugar paste (see pages 140–145)

8 tablespoons white royal icing (see pages 130–133)

16 sheets of edible gold leaf

14 Hand-moulded White Sugar Paste Roses (see pages 196–198)

30 green holly leaves (see page 199)

1 Hand-moulded Amaryllis (see pages 204–205)

400g (14oz) white sugar paste, for blocking

FOR THE BERRIES (MAKES 30)

115g (4oz) red sugar paste (see page 144)

4 tablespoons edible red glitter

YOU WILL ALSO NEED

27.5cm (11 inch) cake board, lined with white sugar paste

Impression star rolling pin

1.5m (5ft) green ribbon

Piping bag fitted with a No. 2 nozzle

Scribe/pokey tool

Little Venice Cake Company template (see page 263)

28-gauge wire

3 x Ribbon Loops (see pages 244–245)

White floristry tape

Dowelling rods – 6–8 for the 2 base tiers

Polystyrene block

3m (10ft) of 25mm (1 inch) red ribbon

3m (10ft) of 15mm (¾ inch) red ribbon

Begin by covering the cakes and lining the board. Run an impression pin over the lined board to impart a textured design and add the green ribbon. Leave to set overnight. All tiers must be decorated before stacking.

Fill a piping bag fitted with a No.2 nozzle with white royal icing and pipe a crown garland design around the top tier cake (see pages 170–171).

Apply gold leaf to the entire middle tier following the instructions on pages 254–255.

Use a scribe/pokey tool to prick the Little Venice Cake Company template design around the sides of the base tier. Fill a piping bag fitted with a No.2 nozzle with white royal icing and pipe on the lace design. Leave all tiers to dry overnight.

Meanwhile, make the decorations. Make the roses, leaves and amaryllis flower as shown on pages 196–199 and 204–205.

Make 30 red glitter berries by rolling red sugar paste into pea-sized balls and dropping them into a bowl of red edible glitter. Insert a 10cm (4 inch) length of 28-guage wire into 8–10 of the berries (leaving the rest loose to be added with the white roses) and leave to dry overnight. Make the ribbon loops.

Once dry, tape up the amaryllis, ribbon loops and wired red berries with white floristry tape ready to top the cake.

Dowel the base tier (see pages 158–159) with a 2.5cm (1 inch) polystyrene block. Top with the middle and top tiers stacked centrally (see pages 154–155). Edge all of the tiers with both thicknesses of ribbon (see page 149).

Fix a sausage of sugar paste around the polystyrene block and use it to fix roses, holly leaves and red glitter berries into position using white royal icing to secure them.

Fix the top decoration in position with white royal icing or insert a posy pick into the cake and fix the corsage into this held in place with royal icing.

Cake Templates

I have included all the templates you will need to recreate my cakes and cookies with a professional finish. Photocopy these pages or trace them as you need them.

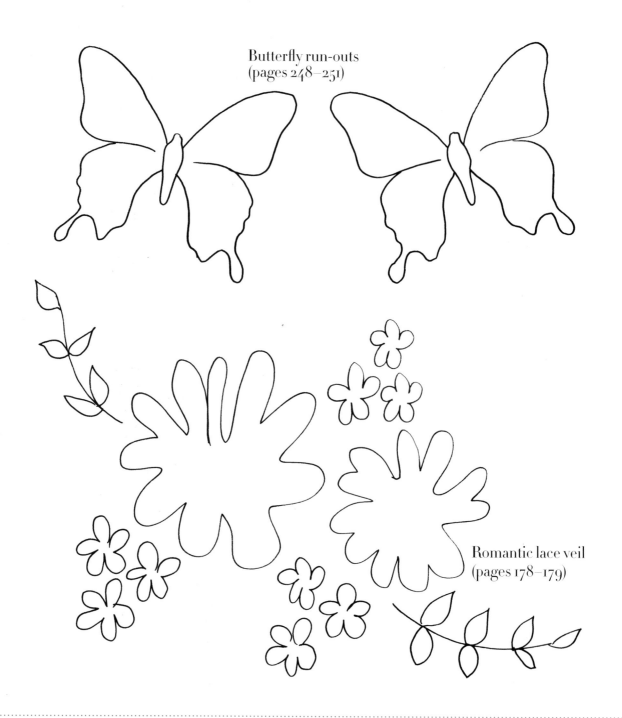

Butterfly run-outs
(pages 248–251)

Romantic lace veil
(pages 178–179)

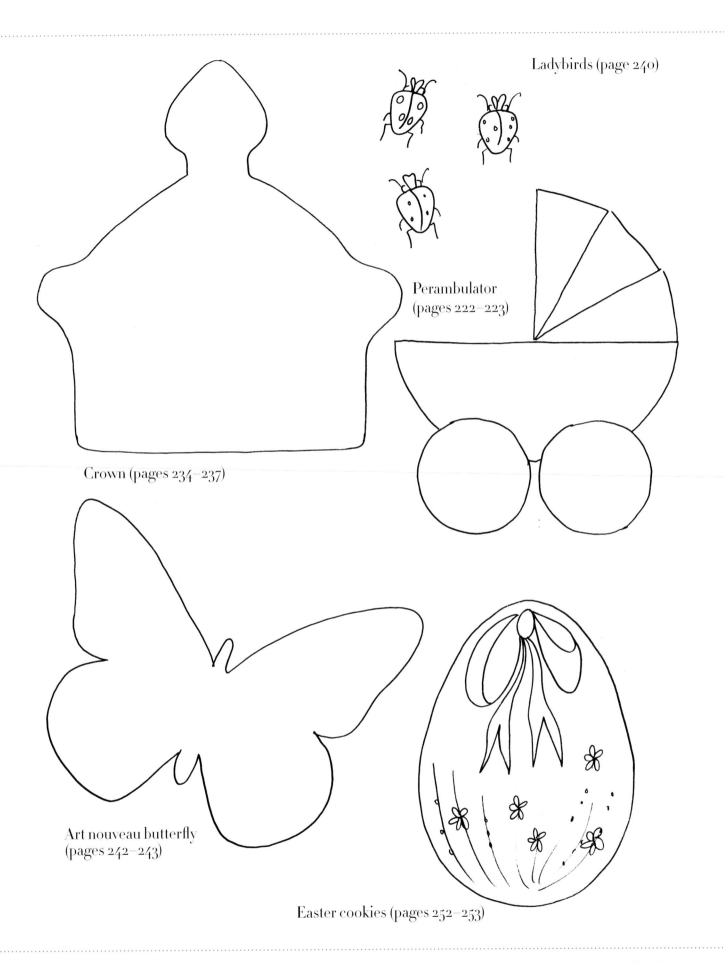

Ladybirds (page 240)

Perambulator
(pages 222–223)

Crown (pages 234–237)

Art nouveau butterfly
(pages 242–243)

Easter cookies (pages 252–253)

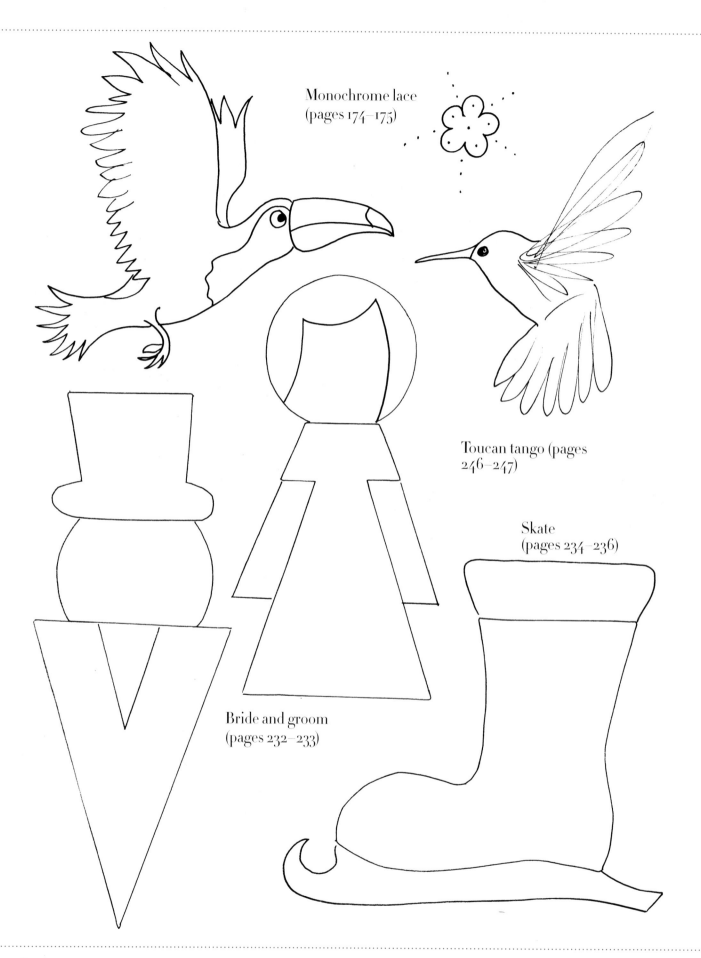

Monochrome lace
(pages 174–175)

Toucan tango (pages
246–247)

Skate
(pages 234–236)

Bride and groom
(pages 232–233)

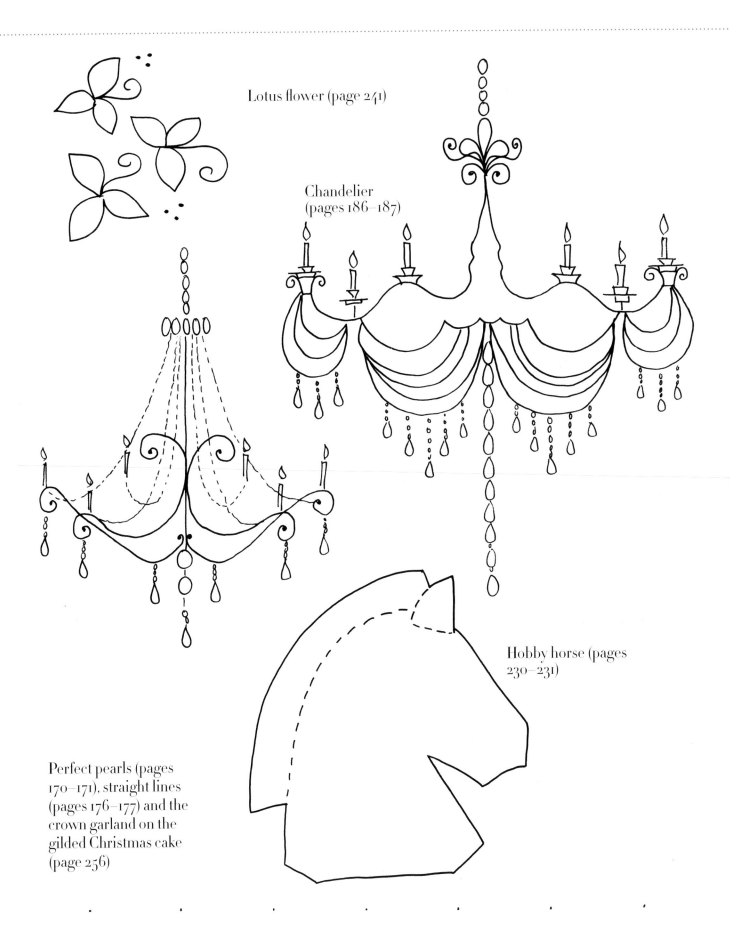

Lotus flower (page 241)

Chandelier
(pages 186–187)

Hobby horse (pages
230–231)

Perfect pearls (pages
170–171), straight lines
(pages 176–177) and the
crown garland on the
gilded Christmas cake
(page 256)

Granny's tiara
(pages 184–185)

Straight lines
(pages 176–177)

Daisy quilt (pages 188–189)

Little Venice Cake Company™ lace
(pages 180–181 and 256–257)

TOOLS

A competent craftsman never blames his tools – as long as he has the right tools for the job! These are the tools I deem necessary for a professional finish. There are many cutters – shapes, flowers, leaves and so on – that can be used to extend your repertoire once these basics have been mastered.

WEIGHTS AND MEASURES

Invest in accurate scales that can weigh powders, solids and liquids in metric and imperial – these are the most versatile and take up little space in the cupboard.

Measuring spoons and cups
These are essential for accurate measurements of spices and raising agents. I like the sets that can be separated for ease of use and cleaning, but joined back together for safe keeping. Spoons should range from a pinch to 1 tablespoon. Cups make it easier to follow recipes with American measurements and are always handy to have in the kitchen.

Measuring jugs
Useful for measuring and transporting liquids such as fruit juices, eggs, oil, milk and cream. I like to use jugs that can be heated in a microwave and have various measurements clearly listed on the side.

PREPARATION

Mixing bowls
Have various sizes to accommodate the task in hand. They need to be large enough to allow for the size of mix and adequate aeration, small enough to accommodate a variety of ingredients. I like the benefit of pyrex, plastic and china that can be heated and chilled. Stainless steel bowls with a rounded base increase the surface area and are a good heat conductor so are particularly good for making ganache and heat-treated meringues. Ensure you have plenty of bowls to aid with preparation. It is helpful to have a selection of sealable airtight containers and tubs for prepared fillings and frostings, icings and sauces.

Spatulas
Used for spooning, mixing, cleaning bowls. Have a few different sizes, including silicone ones that are dishwasher safe.

Spoons
Metal spoons are for folding and accurate measuring, wooden spoons for mixing and creaming.

Ladles
For sauces and ganaches, accurate spooning and a clean professional finish.

Graters / microplane
For superfine grating and zesting of vegetables, fruits, chocolate and spices.

Knives
Large serrated knives with a semi flexible, tapered blade are essential to professionally trim cakes and slice them in preparation for buttercreams and frostings.

Palette knives – straight-handled and crank-handled palette knives of different sizes can be used to paddle buttercreams and frostings between layers of cake and to skim coat to achieve a smooth, professional finish. Smaller palette knives are perfect for the more delicate tasks – buttercreaming smaller cakes and lifting delicate decorations into place.

Small paring knives – perfect for trimming marzipan and sugar paste as they are semi flexible and sharp. I use these for cutting intricate detail on decorations – or even use a craft knife.

Chopping knives – for fruits, nuts, chocolate, spices and butter.

CAKE MAKING

Whisks
Invest in an electric mixer with different attachments that allow for creaming and whisking. I like to have a second bowl available for flexibility and a beater with a rubber spatula edge included to scrape the entire bowl as it beats.

Hand-held electric whisks – practical for whisking 'remotely' for example over a bain marie when making a whisked method cake, heated meringue and buttercreams.

Balloon whisks – useful for hand-whisking cream and adding air if mixing and beating buttercreams. They are useful when making ganache, heating jams or caramels.

Sieves and strainers
Large fine-mesh sieves – perfect for sifting flours and icing sugars to aerate, remove lumps and mix ingredients together in the case of flours, spices and raising agents. They are also useful for passing fruit purées and citrus curds through to remove seeds and lumps.

Smaller tea strainers – perfect for passing fruit juices such as lemon juice when making royal icing.

Tins
There are so many tins available – non-stick, heavy-duty, shaped, loose-bottomed, silicone, trays, springform – it can be daunting to know where to start:

- Heavy-duty round and square tins in various sizes from 10cm (4 inches) to 40cm (16 inches) and loaf tins – these really are the backbone of your kitchen. Look for lightweight, anodized aluminium with rigid, straight sides (not tapered), at least 7.5cm (3 inches) baking depth, with no seams, that can be easily cleaned (or better still be suitable for the dishwasher). These will ensure the heat conducts evenly and quickly, ensuring an even bake on the cake. They stack inside each other for easy storage.

- Non-stick and shaped cake tins – these are suitable for fresh baked cakes that are intended to be eaten straightaway. Kugelhopfs and tube pans should still be greased with a quick-release spray to allow for easy removal of cakes.

- Springform tins and loose-bottomed tins are good for delicate cakes which require careful handling when removing them from the tins – such as whisked cakes.

- **Roulades** should be baked in rectangular, shallow-sided, angular tins, lined with non-stick baking parchment.
- **Bun or muffin tins** should always be lined with paper cases – they simply allow the cases to be supported and transported with ease.

Baking paper and paper cases

I like to line my tins with non-stick baking parchment. This is available in sheets or on a roll which can be cut to size for a one-time use, making it hygienic but expensive.

Cupcakes and muffins can be baked in decorative paper cases and tulip wraps. There are many available to personalise the cakes and bakes your are making.

Ready-shaped liners for specific tins can be a time saver if you are batch baking the same size cakes on a regular basis.

Bake-O-Glide – this is a heat-resistant, reusable, washable non-stick baking sheet that can be cut to size to fit each tin and reused. It can be a good long-term investment.

Cooling racks

Round or square, some racks can even be tiered and stacked for batch baking. Ensure they are kept scrupulously clean. They are used for cooling cakes and when pouring chocolate ganache or fondant.

Cake tester

This is a metal skewer which can be inserted into the centre of a cake while it is in the oven to see if it is baked. It can also be used to skewer the cake prior to a syrup being poured or ladled over the cake.

Pastry brush

Flat head or round head brushes are useful in the kitchen for applying jam to a cake, or brushing marzipan with brandy before applying sugar paste. They are used for brushing melted chocolate.

FILLINGS, FROSTING AND ICINGS

Rolling pins

Invest in a series of rolling pins of different sizes and lengths suitable for specific tasks.

Long (60cm/24 inch) rolling pins make light work of rolling out marzipan and sugar paste.

Medium-sized rolling pins (30–35cm/12–14 inch) are perfect for cookie dough.

Small rolling pins (15–20cm/6-8 inch) are ideal for rolling petal paste or sugar paste for refined decorations and sugar flowers.

Icing sugar dusters

I have several of these filled with different powders – cocoa, icing sugar, unrefined icing sugar – to allow for superfine dusting of work surfaces and dusting fresh baked cakes with ease. They deliver a controlled, sifted dusting.

Impression rolling pins (image)

There are many acrylic impression pins available which should be used after regular rolling of icing. They apply an embossed or indented detail perfect for lining boards, or for cutting out shapes which can be applied to cakes and cookies.

ASSEMBLY

Acrylic work boards

It is essential to have a series of working boards – for splitting cakes and supporting cakes while you are working on them. I have a set of round and square, acrylic, super thin but rigid boards, which are all suitable for the freezer and dishwasher. They can even be separated with pillars or supports for a ready made display stand.

Cake boards or drums

These are available as round, square, petal, hexagonal, octagonal, heart or rectangular shapes. They are constructed from a 12mm (½ inch) thickness of dense card wrapped in either silver, gold or coloured foil. A top tip is to write the size on the base as you buy them. I tend to line most of my cake boards with sugar paste before edging in 15mm ribbon.

Thinner cake boards or cards are available, which are fine for cakes which are going to be further supported on a larger lined cake drum, but not for stacking cakes. They are not durable enough and the cakes are prone to sagging underneath the weight.

Dowelling rods

These are essential for successfully tiering cakes to offer internal support. They are used to even the tiers and ensure the tiers do not sink. They are made from a food safe plastic which can be snapped easily once scored with heavy-duty scissors or cut all the way through or trimmed with a junior hacksaw. They come in extra long lengths if required for supporting deep cakes and pillars.

Pillars

Traditionally made of plaster of Paris but now more commonly plastic or acrylic, pillars are used to separate tiers to add height. They can be from 8–30cm (3–12 inches) in height. Pillars used on a royal-iced cake do not necessarily need to be dowelled as the royal icing is very stiff and supportive. In my experience and for peace of mind, I tend to dowel every tier inside the pillars.

DECORATING

Turntables

I think it is essential to have a higher turntable with a smaller diameter (20cm/8 inch) for working on individual or single tier cakes; and a larger lower larger diameter (30cm/12 inch) turntable for multi-tier stacked cakes for ease of decoration.

Round cutters

I use a set of 3 concentric stainless steel cutters for making the individual or 'crown' cakes. The smaller cuts out the cake, the middle is for trimming the marzipan and the larger for trimming the sugar paste. These ensure all the cakes are uniform and even.

Smoothers

Icing and marzipan smoothers offer a professional finish to covered celebration cakes. They smooth the paste to create a flawless finish. Round edge smoothers are used for the top and sides of the cake. Right-angled or straight edge smoothers are used on the base of the side of the cake or for smoothing crown cakes.

Pizza wheel or rotary cutter

This is a great tool for cutting marzipan or sugar paste where it is important not to stretch or pull the paste – such as cutting out squares for covering individual cakes.

Thermometer

Sugar thermometers are useful for accurately recording the temperature of sugar syrups and chocolate when making meringue, citrus curds, praline or tempering chocolate.

Piping bags

I tend to make my disposable icing piping bags from non-stick baking parchment, held in place with a staple. Larger piping bags for cupcakes, cream-based frostings and ganache should be plastic – either disposable (hygienic) or reusable cloth bags with a siliconized lining (which must be scrupulously cleaned after use).

Nozzles
Larger stainless steel nozzles are perfect for buttercreams and ganaches. Smaller nozzles are reserved for the more refined hand piping with royal icing or melted chocolate for hand piping messages.

Nozzle cleaner
An essential handy little brush tool for scrupulously cleaning those little tricky icing nozzles.

Modelling tools and scribes
Modelling tools are useful for applying professional touches to hand-moulded sugar flowers and models. They include, but are not limited to:

Ball tool: for shaping flowers and applying paw prints on model animals.

Smiley tool: adding smiles to characters.

Cone: for shaping pulled flowers, adding ears and eye sockets to model animals.

Stitching tool: a rotary tool for adding a decorative stitching detail to modelled decorations.

Shell: adding shell detail.

Star: adding indented stars.

Blade: precision detail.

Scribe or pokey tool: stencilling and transcribing templates and messages onto cakes.

Paint palette, paints, brushes
Invest in a multi-welled paint palette that can hold a number of colours, dusts and lustres. Have a selection of paintbrushes for larger strokes and finer detail.

Lustre sprays, colours and dusts, shimmers and glitters
These add the finishing touches to your cake decorations and detail:

Metallic lustre sprays – I find clear, gold, pearl and silver a good selection to have in the store cupboard.

Colour gels – use the concentrated edible gels to colour sugar paste, petal or gum paste, royal icing and buttercreams.

Colour dusts – colour dusts blend well with cocoa butter or rejuvenating spirit for painting – select a good palette of colours and always include black and white.

Shimmers and glitters
These are available in many colours and sizes. Ensure they are edible (made from sugar) if they are intended to be consumed. Store in airtight containers away from moisture to prevent clumping.

Gold leaf
Available in sheets in a book interleaved with non-stick paper or as nuggets in jars. It is important to keep gold leaf away from moisture or it will stick and not handle easily.

Chocolate freeze spray
This pressurized canister of freeze spray is invaluable when working with chocolate. One quick blast will instantly freeze melted chocolate. Made from tetrafluoroethane and available commercially.

Flower cutters, veiners, leaf cutters
These are extensive. Invest in a series of 5-petal cutters, a lily cutter and veiner and a series of leaf veiners and cutters and add to these as you build up your repertoire of sugar flowers.

Plastic pouch
I use a simple A4 stationery document pouch cut open along the 2 closed sides to create a pouch for making all my hand moulded roses and rose buds using sugar paste, petal paste and modelling chocolate.

Cookie cutters and shapes
Hearts, stars, flowers and crowns are very useful for cookies as well as crown cake decorations. Store them in sealed tub, labelled so you can always find them easily! If you can't find the shape you want, draw it on card and cut out your own template.

Wires
These are available in green, white or a rainbow of colours and even foil. Used for flowers, ribbon loops, wiring stars and other decorations or simply for curling and adding to a wired corsage of flowers.

Ribbons
Double satin, grosgrain, organza, patterned, wired – don't underestimate the instant transformation of a cake with a ribbon. Our one ribbon drawer has grown now to six! Use a food safe or coated ribbon if it is coming into direct contact with a cake.

Scissors
I have task scissors – ribbon scissors just for ribbon to keep them super sharp.

Multi-purpose scissors
For general tasks and trimming non-stick baking parchment.

Heavy-duty scissors
For trimming wires and dowelling rods.

Invaluable stationery tools
Pencil: for marking dowelling rods and tracing for painted designs.

Ruler: for measuring and drawing lines and marks for templates.

Permanent superfine black marker pen: for drawing all templates onto tracing paper so the pen will not mark the cake.

Tool box
For storage of all your ready-to-hand utensils.

Cake stands
I collect these whenever I find them on my travels. Different shapes, colours and sizes will certainly transform your cakes for a professional finish.

Cake knives, slices
These all add to the finished detail.

INDEX